THE ORIGINS OF THE
AMERICAN PARTY SYSTEM

harper ⚱ torchbooks

*A reference-list of Harper Torchbooks, classified
by subjects, is printed at the end of this volume.*

THE ORIGINS OF THE
AMERICAN
PARTY SYSTEM

THREE ESSAYS

by JOSEPH CHARLES

Foreword by FREDERICK MERK

HARPER TORCHBOOKS ❧ THE ACADEMY LIBRARY

Harper & Row, Publishers, New York

Foreword

Joseph E. Charles, the author of these essays, had the command of more than high research skills for his study of Jeffersonian Democracy. He was equipped, as a result of his own family background, with an intuitive understanding of the problems and meanings of Jeffersonian Democracy. His forebears were a race of pioneers. They were part of that westward movement of which Jefferson was part, and of which his political crusade was an eighteenth-century manifestation. As early as the close of the seventeenth century Charleses were to be found living in the first restless frontier settlements of North Carolina. Succeeding generations were presently flowing westward along routes which Southern migrants—including the family of Abraham Lincoln—followed into the Old Northwest. In what is now Indiana some of them found root, and there, at Talbot, in the western part of the state, on August 9, 1906, Joseph Charles was born. It is from this background that his interest in Jeffersonian Democracy emerged and also the intellectual fibre distinguishing him—the rugged realism, the keen perceptiveness, and the democratic idealism that are reflected in these essays.

His education was partly Middle Western, partly Eastern. He took his undergraduate degree and a Master's degree in English Literature at the University of Illinois; his Master's degree and Ph.D. in History at Harvard. His graduate education was financed by teaching at the University of Illinois, at the secondary-school level, and finally at Harvard. For four years he was a teaching fellow at Harvard on the staff of the survey course in European History then known as History 1. He proved an exceptionally stimulating and devoted teacher, remembered with esteem by his students. His dissertation was on the subject of the Party Origins of Jeffersonian Democracy. It was a brilliant piece of original analysis.

The labor of preparing it for publication was interrupted by the Second World War. For ten years Charles was in the service of the United States government—from 1942 to 1952. He served with the Office of Strategic Services and the U. S. Marine Corps Reserve in London. In 1945 he joined the Department of State in Washington. In 1947 he served as Cultural

Attaché at the U. S. Embassy in London for a time and then was made a First Secretary. His great interest during these years was in interpreting the United States to the British people, and here his background was of the greatest use. Already during the war, he had given voluntary service on a mixed panel of British and Americans which met at various military posts and held informal public discussions about the United States, the war, and the coming settlement. Both in Britain and in the United States he had much to do with the setting up of the exchange-of-persons programs which were started after the war. In 1951 he returned to Washington and, having decided to make Foreign Service his career, he passed the Foreign Service examinations in early November of 1952. Only about two weeks later he was killed in a Washington street accident on November 21, 1952.

His years of service to the nation were years of a growing output in studies in our early national history. Many of the findings in the thesis were, while their author was in federal service, rediscovered and published by others. The thesis, which would have been proclaimed a major historical contribution, if published in 1942, seemed to its author an unfinished work which he always hoped he would sometime be able to refine and strengthen.

The volume here published consists of chapters selected from the thesis. The chapters chosen were those found most nearly in finished form and those most nearly retaining the freshness and newness that had once marked the whole. They were selected and edited by Douglass Adair and Lawrence Towner for *The William and Mary Quarterly,* where they appeared as separate articles in the April, July, and October numbers of 1955. They were put through the press with the help of Dr. Charles's widow, Mary Louise Foster Charles. Their republication in book form is at once a fitting memorial to a distinguished scholar and a contribution to the world of scholarship.

FREDERICK MERK

Contents

THE ORIGINS OF THE
AMERICAN PARTY SYSTEM

I

Hamilton and Washington

1. THE MEN OF THE REVOLUTION

THE leading political figures of the 1790's had been active in public life at least twenty years; but after 1789, the men of the Revolution faced a final task, one upon which the success and meaning of their earlier labors depended. The winning of independence and the framing and adoption of the Constitution would be of little importance if the men who had shared in these achievements were to be unable to live together harmoniously. These men had to adapt an untried instrument of government to a new country, and it is the last phase of the political education and experience of the men of the Revolution which we study when we follow the main theme of American history from 1789 to 1801.

The 1790's were for a good many of these men a more trying period than any they had yet experienced, for wide and bitter differences gradually developed among them. Many of the points at issue were of such fundamental importance that posterity also has divided upon them; and, through partisanship and by assumptions based on later developments of our history, later treatments have tended to echo rather than to explain the conflict of the period. The contest of later parties for the sanction of one or the other of the Founding Fathers has given us a false perspective, and has caused us to emphasize, not the problems which faced the leading figures in the 1790's and not the courses which they followed in solving them, but rather the rationalizations and the propaganda by which they sought to justify themselves and win support. Thus the figures of this period are tagged and labeled for us in advance. We are likely to think of their conduct from 1789 to 1801 as predetermined by temperament, by economic interest, or by sectional loyalty, and to assume that the resulting divisions existed, at least in the germ, before the issues arose. Of some men this supposition is doubtless true; but probably a greater number might very easily have taken positions precisely opposite to those which they actually did take had the decisive issues been presented only a little differently. In dealing with a question as complicated as the basis of party division, we need to emphasize the importance of what H. A. L. Fisher has called "the play of the contingent and the unforeseen."[1] If we approach the study of this period wearing the blinders of a determinism of any kind, we are likely to overlook what is perhaps the most important element in any crowded, busy historical scene. The milieu, in part made up by the flow of events and the questions at issue, but also giving these their color, demands our constant attention; for it, and not the background of later generations, determined the way in which the men of the 1790's viewed the urgent problems of the new government.

Enjoying the prestige if not all the privileges of aristocrats, many of this generation thought that they were building a society in which the benefits heretofore reserved for the few would be more widely distributed. The most conservative among them had views and assumptions which would have astounded a European. Yet this was a legalistic generation, very touchy on the subject of their rights and with a deep respect for law. They did not regard their Revolution as a break with the past, nor did they ignore precedent and experience in forming their new government. They aimed rather at a new synthesis, under auspicious circumstances, of the best that was known in the theory and practice of government. Their curious mixture of close regard for the past and boundless hope for the future is shown in Washington's circular letter to the governors, written in 1783 at the end of the Revolution:

. . . The foundation of our Empire was not laid in the gloomy age of Ignorance and Superstition, but at an Epocha when the rights of mankind were better understood and more clearly defined, than at any former period, the researches of the human mind, after social happiness, have been carried to a great extent, the Treasures of knowledge, acquired by the labours of Philosophers, Sages and Legislatures, through a long succession of years, are laid open for our use, and their collected wisdom may be happily applied in the

---

[1] "One intellectual excitement has, however, been denied me. Men wiser and more learned than I have discerned in history a plot, a rhythm, a predetermined pattern. These harmonies are concealed from me. I can see only one emergency following upon another as wave follows upon wave, only one great fact with respect to which, since it is unique, there can be no generalizations, only one safe rule for the historian: that he should recognize in the development of human destinies the play of the contingent and the unforeseen." Herbert Albert Laurens Fisher, *A History of Europe* (Boston and New York, 1935-36), Preface, vii.

Establishment of our forms of Government. . . . At this auspicious period, the United States came into existence as a Nation, and if their Citizens should not be completely free and happy, the fault will be intirely their own.[2]

This is in the authentic vein of the generation of the Revolution, though in the 1790's many, perhaps Washington himself, would have regarded such language as visionary.

If we are to credit their most solemn assertions, all the more eminent figures wished to escape from the public life which was the only outlet for the peculiar training and genius of most of them. Yet a Hamilton, a Jefferson, a Burr, an Adams out of public life seems to us like a fish trying to leave water. Precocious all in what Aristotle called the most difficult of the arts, several of this generation pursued their peculiar mixture of intellectual and political activity over an amazing span of years. Young in the 1790's, they grew to the stature of their tasks and obstacles; and during the following decades, as the many aspects of the problem of how to govern well present themselves, we see a greater profusion of talents dedicated to its solution than history has recorded elsewhere.[3]

During the 1790's the country was absorbed not so much in recuperating from the Revolution as in determining and carrying out its logical conclusions. Most of the attention paid to these men as a group has been concentrated upon their activities during the Revolution and at the time of the framing and adoption of the Constitution. Though at these times sharp differences arose among them, nevertheless co-operation and concession may be regarded as the keynote of both achievements. We, on the other hand, study them at a time when the cynical might say that they were fighting over the spoils, and when any honest observer must report

[2] Circular to the states, Headquarters, Newburgh, Jun. 8, 1783, J. C. Fitzpatrick, ed., *The Writings of George Washington from the Original Manuscript Sources, 1777-1805*, 39 vols. (Washington, 1931-44), XXVI, 485. Hereafter cited as Fitzpatrick, *Washington's Writings.*

[3] Samuel Eliot Morison states that he and Harold Laski agreed "that with the sole exception of England of the Commonwealth, no community in modern history has been so fecund in political thought, as America in the revolutionary generation." William Manning, *The Key of Libberty* (notes and a foreword by Samuel Eliot Morison, Billerica, Massachusetts, 1922), Introduction, xiv. [Editor's note. *The Key of Libberty* was reprinted in the *William and Mary Quarterly*, 3rd Ser., XIII (1956), 202-254.] As far as political theory is concerned, perhaps this group of men should not take precedence over all others. They had had, however, more practical experience in constructing and operating governments, when we consider the establishment of the state governments, than had been the lot of seventeenth-century Englishmen.

more of dissension and bitterness than of agreement. We hear much of eighteenth-century optimism, and the achievements of this generation would have warranted it, but we are studying a period when thoughtful men were frequently subject to apprehension and despair. All reflecting people were oppressed by the fact that the danger in the later years arose primarily not from a foreign invader, but from former comrades-in-arms or fellow-legislators. Each side, as the division grew wider, came to regard the other as traitors to the common cause of their earlier years. The group that had traveled so far together as a reasonably compact band came to the main fork in the road, not with the framing and adoption of the Constitution, but during the 1790's. How to administer machinery newly set up, what concrete meaning, in unforeseen contingencies, to give to words which no longer meant the same thing to all: these were the new problems which weakened old ties and sharpened earlier differences.

These men had no narrow conception of their differences; they thought in terms of "fixing the national character"[4] and of choosing the path the new nation should follow. James Madison is said to have observed at the Constitutional Convention "that it is more than probable we are now digesting a plan which in its operation will decide forever the fate of Republican government." Madison was not alone in this view. Men who felt that the future of republicanism depended upon the operation of a government based on a document so full of compromises as our Constitution were bound to divide on practical questions. No matter what the nature of the Constitution, however, wide and bitter divisions were inevitable at this time; for the fundamental issue of the 1790's was no other than what form of government and what type of society were to be produced in this country. Many thought that the conduct of this country would determine the outcome of the struggle in Europe,[5] and that world as well as national history thus waited upon their efforts. Thus the taste of this generation for grandeur and sublimity found expression

---

[4] The election of 1800, "they [the Republicans] appeared to believe, would 'fix our national character' and 'determine whether republicanism or aristocracy' should prevail. Moreover, the solution of this problem in America might 'perhaps turn the suspended balance in favor of liberty or despotism throughout the world.'" See "Address by the Committee of Essex County to the People of New Jersey," in *New Jersey Journal*, Aug. 19, 1800, quoted by Walter Ray Fee, *The Transition from Aristocracy to Democracy in New Jersey, 1789-1829* (Somerville, New Jersey, 1933), 100.

[5] *Ibid.*

in the struggles of their political life, and the great figures, perhaps many of the humble, were conscious that they were living an epic.

2. ALEXANDER HAMILTON

The characters of Burr and Jefferson are supposed to be the great puzzles of the early national period. Jefferson is held up in general text-books on American history as the classic example of inconsistency, of departure in office from principles laid down while in opposition. Yet neither of these men is more puzzling, if we raise the question of ultimate purposes, than is Hamilton, and neither appears more inconsistent than Hamilton if we put some of his most important words and actions side by side.

In Numbers 12 and 21 of *The Federalist* Hamilton all but promised his readers that no excise or land tax would be levied under the new Constitution.[6] Yet an excise was an early part of the economic program, and from 1795 on, he was advocating policies which could only be paid for by a land tax.[7]

Generally regarded as the high priest of sound and conservative finan-cial policies, Hamilton was apparently untroubled by the condition of our paper money in 1795-96,[8] which, taken with our general financial

[6] Vols. XI, XII of Henry Cabot Lodge, ed., *The Works of Alexander Hamilton,* 12 vols. (New York, 1904), hereafter cited as Lodge, *Hamilton's Works,* contain *The Federalist.* For Hamilton's promise on the excises, see *Federalist* 12, *ibid.,* XI, 92; on land taxes, see *Federalist* 12, 21, *ibid.,* 92, 166.

[7] Though Hamilton in *Federalist* 12 explained that no excise would be levied because the "genius of the people" hated excises, he seems to have welcomed the rebellion against his excise as an occasion for displaying the military power of the state. Leland DeWitt Baldwin, in his book *Whiskey Rebels* (Pittsburgh, 1939), does not say what he believes to have been Hamilton's motives in forcing the issue on the matter of the Excise in 1794, but he gives evidence which would support the conclu-sion that for political reasons Hamilton was glad of the opportunity to crush resistance to central government by force at that particular time. See especially pp. 110-12, 184, 220-21, 234-35. On p. 269 he states, "If Hamilton was actually trying to pacify the West the circumstances surrounding the issuance of the processes served in July, 1794, certainly showed political ineptitude; an accusation not lightly to be made against him."

[8] See correspondence for those years between Hamilton and Oliver Wolcott, Secretary of the Treasury, in George Gibbs, ed., *Memoirs of the Administrations of Washington and John Adams* (New York, 1846), hereafter cited as Gibbs, *Memoirs;* John Church Hamilton, ed., *The Works of Alexander Hamilton,* 7 vols. (New York, 1850-51), hereafter cited as Hamilton, *Hamilton's Works;* Hamilton Papers, Library of Congress, hereafter cited as Hamilton Papers, LC. Wolcott was greatly disturbed by our financial condition at this time. See Wolcott to Hamilton, Dec. 8, 1796, Hamilton, *Hamilton's Works,* VI, 175-76.

condition at that time, seemed even to Federalists to constitute a dangerous problem.[9] A little later he appears to have been urging fiat money as a means of helping the government out of its financial difficulties; for in August, 1798, he wrote to Wolcott, the Secretary of the Treasury:

For these and other reasons [scarcity of money for the interior needs of the government], which I have thought well of, I have come to the conclusion, that our Treasury ought to raise up a circulation of its own. I mean by the issuing of Treasury notes payable, some on demand, others at different periods, from very short to pretty considerable,—at first having but little time to run. . . .[10]

The only assiduous pamphleteer among the public figures of the first order at that time, and a man who had been more important in helping to finance and direct partisan newspapers than any other leader in either party, Hamilton wrote in 1802, ". . . they [the Federalists] erred in relying so much on the rectitude and utility of their measures as to have neglected the cultivation of popular favor, by fair and justifiable expedients."[11]

In *Federalist* 11 Hamilton had written, "Let Americans disdain to be the instruments of European greatness! Let the thirteen States, bound together in a strict indissoluble Union, concur in erecting one great American system, superior to the control of all transatlantic force or influence, and able to dictate the terms of the connection between the old and the new world!"[12] Yet during the negotiation and the struggle for the ratification of the Jay Treaty, as during the years 1798-99, Hamilton must at least have thought our interests inseparable from Great Britain's and our support to be had on her own terms, if he did not, as his opponents charged, put her interest above that of this country.[13]

On the question of the ability of the American people to govern themselves and of the part that they were to have in the new government,

---

[9] John Adams to his wife, Philadelphia, Feb. 15, 1796. "The money of the country, the paper money, is the most unpleasant object I see. This must have a remedy, and I fear it will be western rebellion, or the opposition to the treaty." Charles Francis Adams, *Letters of John Adams. Addressed to His Wife*, 2 vols. (Boston, 1841), II, 202. See below, p. 242, for Wolcott's letter showing the way in which he viewed our situation.

[10] Hamilton to Wolcott, New York, Aug. 22, 1798, Hamilton, *Hamilton's Works*, VI, 349.

[11] *Ibid.*, 541.

[12] Lodge, *Hamilton's Works*, XI, 88.

[13] See below, The Jay Treaty, part 2.

many of Hamilton's utterances from 1787 to 1789 were in sharp conflict with his later words and policies. In a speech at the New York Constitutional Convention he said:

. . . We have been told that the old Confederation has proved inefficacious, only because intriguing and powerful men, aiming at revolution, have been for ever instigating the people and rendering them disaffected to it. This, sir, is a false insinuation.

I will venture to assert that no combination of designing men under heaven will be capable of making a government unpopular which is in its principles a wise and good one, and vigorous in its application.[14]

Earlier in the same speech he had stated:

After all, we must submit to this idea, that the true principle of a republic is that the people should choose whom they please to govern them. Representation is imperfect in proportion as the current of popular favor is checked. This great source of free government, popular election, should be perfectly pure, and the most unbounded liberty allowed.[15]

Yet as soon as there was popular opposition to any of his measures, Hamilton claimed that it was stirred up by men who wanted to destroy the government. A combination of designing men was his favorite explanation for the opposition to government policies which began to appear by 1793.[16] In practice he believed in free elections no longer than they supported his policies, for in 1800 he tried to nullify the popular vote. At that time the practical issue was not only that which Mr. Allen Johnson stated, the question whether or not a political opposition was to be allowed to exist.[17] The more important point was whether or not, when a political opposition had been successful at the polls, the choice of the voters was to be followed. Hamilton appeared willing to go to any lengths to circumvent the popular vote in 1800 when he saw that the Federalists would be defeated by following it.[18]

[14] Lodge, *Hamilton's Works*, II, 29.
[15] *Ibid.*, II, 27-8; XI, 308-09; XII, 91-2.
[16] *Ibid.*, V, 190-91.
[17] "For a season it seemed as though the Republican party was to be denied the right to exist as a legal opposition, entitled to obtain power by persuasion. . . . They [the Republicans] won, therefore, for all time that recognition of the right of legal opposition which is the primary condition of successful popular government." Allen Johnson, *Union and Democracy* (Boston and New York, 1915), 119.
[18] Stephen Van Rensselaer to Hamilton, Albany, Mar. 15, 1799. "The Assembly

Such contradictions and inconsistencies as these are not of great importance except as they reflect the fundamental problem which is raised by contrasting Hamilton's general views on government with the policies which he followed. While the Constitution was being adopted, no one spoke of the interest of the whole country or of the necessity for concessions by every group, interest, and section more persuasively than did Hamilton. It was his pride that he was able to "think continentally." Yet the High-Federalist measures from 1796 to 1800, which were only the last of a series of steps that had narrowed the base of Federalist support and had made the party hated over large sections of the country, were those of a body of men who looked to him for leadership. It seems likely that a study of Hamilton which was based directly upon what he did or tried to do would be very different from one based upon his writings or the customary accounts of him.

Among the fundamental problems raised by a study of Hamilton's political behavior is the question whether his contributions to *The Federalist* represent his ideas of the way in which the new government would operate, or whether these essays were merely clever propaganda for the adoption of the Constitution. Did Hamilton in the years from 1787 to 1789 envisage a nation unified in sentiment by mutual concessions, by a genuine concern for the interests of the whole, as some passages of *The Federalist* might lead one to believe? Did he really believe in the representative government and free popular elections of which he spoke so favorably in the

---

have a bill for electing Electors of the President & Vice-President—it will pass—are you of the opinion that it would be proper for the Senate to concur? Unless New York gives us a different representation the federalists are lost—Whether we have any object now since the late conduct of the President—you are a better judge than we. If it is however necessary that we should still persevere pray let me hear from you. Our friends are extremely pressing that I should write to you on the subject." Hamilton Papers, LC.

It is generally known that Hamilton wrote to Jay, May 7, 1800, after the Republicans had won the election for the New York State Assembly, urging that Jay call together the old assembly, which was Federalist, and have them choose the electors, even though this procedure would have been contrary to law. In the same letter Hamilton shows that he was depending on the Federalists in the Pennsylvania State Senate to prevent the taking of an electoral vote, which would have been Republican. Lodge, *Hamilton's Works*, X, 371-74.

Federalist efforts to prevent the passage of the law necessary for a choice of electors in New York were known to the Republicans at the time. See John Dawson to Madison, Philadelphia, Dec. 12, 1799, Madison Papers, Library of Congress. Hereafter cited as Madison Papers, LC.

New York Constitutional Convention?[19] Further, did Hamilton's fundamental views and purposes change between 1787 and 1800, or did they
remain the same, concealed part of the time behind a calculated mis-
representation, a clever soothing of "the great beast"? These questions are
important, for Jefferson is supposed to have been the hypocrite, the wily
politician of the time, and Hamilton, whatever his faults, always to have
been frank, open, honest, and manly.

We cannot give a definite answer to these questions, but it is worth-
while recording that Hamilton did not render his lip service, if such it
was, to representative government until after he had tried in the Constitutional Convention to win support for a plan of government which
was only a thinly veiled elective monarchy.[20] When Hamilton found
that he could not win a following for this scheme, he gave the Constitution which was drafted his heartiest support. His enemies later claimed
that he did so only because he hoped that in the right hands the new
government might be made into something which, in operation, would
closely resemble the government he had championed. In 1802 he wrote
a letter to Gouverneur Morris which would imply that he had never had
any faith in the Constitution. He described it as "a frail and worthless
fabric which I have been endeavoring to prop up."[21] Such facts as these
do not necessarily furnish the explanation of Hamilton's policies. They
do not prove the contention of his enemies that he was trying while in
office to bring about a monarchy or a dictatorship. But Hamilton's known
views on government, his open statements to intimates, do raise the question of his fundamental purposes and entitle us to ask whether, for example, the measures of his economic program, so important to the new
nation, were intended to further or subvert the type of government which
most well-informed men thought they were supporting when they voted
to accept the Constitution.

Such fundamental problems as these have not been clarified; they have
not even been set forth by Hamilton's biographers.[22] Thus the standard

[19] See second quotation from Hamilton's speech at the New York Constitutional
Convention, above, p. 9.

[20] Lodge, *Hamilton's Works*, I, 347-69.

[21] Hamilton to G. Morris, Feb. 27, 1802, *ibid.*, X, 425.

[22] William Graham Sumner, *Alexander Hamilton* (New York, 1890); John
Church Hamilton, *The Life of Alexander Hamilton* (Boston, 1879); Henry Cabot
Lodge, *Alexander Hamilton*, in John T. Morse, Jr., ed., *American Statesmen*, VII
(Boston, 1882); Frederick Scott Oliver, *Alexander Hamilton: An Essay on American
Union*, new ed. (New York, 1916).

works on Hamilton evade the main issues which his career raises; and his rightful place in our history, once these issues are raised, becomes a subject for controversy.

Hamilton's whole career invites further study because of his transcendent importance in the forming of our government, but no part of it is of so great importance as that between 1789 and 1800. For those who are interested in the question of party development, his policies and views from 1789 on are probably the most important single problem. If we look at the issues with which public opinion during those years was most concerned and which were the immediate causes of party division, we shall see that there was not one of them in which Hamilton did not play a leading part. The questions were:

1. Should we pass the various measures which made up Hamilton's economic program, 1790-93? [23]

2. Should we declare our neutrality in the war between France and England in 1793, or should we act in accordance with our treaty with France?

3. Should we ratify and put into effect the Jay Treaty?

4. Should we give the Administration crisis powers, 1798-99?

We are for the moment particularly concerned with the first of these crucial questions with which Hamilton was intimately connected. Before going into the details of the various parts of his economic program, however, it is necessary to take a general view of the measures it included and to point out some of their more obvious consequences. When the new government was established, it inherited large debts dating back to the Revolution: debts which were owed to our own citizens, to the French government, and to banking houses in Holland. Under the Articles of

[23] By Hamilton's economic program I mean Funding, Assumption, the Excise Bill, and the bill establishing the Bank. Hamilton's plans for encouraging manufacturing in this country are not treated here. They were not carried out, perhaps because of the mishaps which befell the Society for Establishing Useful Manufactures (see Joseph Stancliffe Davis, *Essays in the Earlier History of American Corporations* [vol. XVI in *Harvard Economic Studies,* Cambridge, 1917], I, 349-504 *passim;* hereafter cited as Davis, *American Corporations*), but it seems more probable that his plans for establishing manufacturing, at least in the near future, were abandoned for other reasons. The change might have come about because a large volume of imports was necessary to maintain government revenue, because Hamilton found himself more dependent for political support on merchants than he had expected to be, or because during the European wars of the early 1790's American capital tended to be engrossed in European trade instead of being invested in the United States.

Confederation we had for some years failed to pay even the interest on some of these debts. In addition to this burden, the states had separate debts which also went back to the Revolution. Some of the states had been as delinquent as Congress in meeting their obligations, while others had made considerable progress in repaying theirs. Hamilton's first step was to fund the national debt, that is, to determine the interest and principal due to each creditor and, since the creditors could not be paid immediately, to issue to them new bonds which were now the basis of the national credit. Although his second step, called Assumption, was included in the Funding Bill as actually passed, it provided for the assuming of the debts of each of the states by the national government, thus, of course, adding to the total of the national debt. His next step was to establish a national bank in which the government owned stock, though it had to go further into debt to acquire this stock.

The main sources of revenue which Hamilton provided for the new government came from indirect taxes on imported goods and from an excise tax laid on liquor made in this country. The choice of these sources of income entailed far-reaching consequences. Since most of our trade was with England and a high volume of imports was necessary for revenues, friendly relations with England became essential to the national credit of the new government. It could not seek a high degree of economic self-sufficiency, nor could it take any diplomatic step which might offend England without grave risks. On the other hand, the Excise Act, as it was passed and administered under Hamilton's influence, brought about the Whiskey Rebellion. As will appear later, there was no point in Hamilton's economic program which is not important for the political as well as for the economic historian. Nowhere do we draw nearer the central issue of the 1790's, the question of what kind of government and society we were to have in this country, than in the study of Hamilton's economic policy.

As we have seen, Hamilton's whole program rested on the funding of the debt, and the manner in which this was done is highly important. The basis of his plan was to issue negotiable bonds to the full amount of the various evidences of indebtedness which would be presented to the national government, without regard to the question of original ownership, the degree of previous depreciation of the security, or the relation between real and nominal value of money at the time that the loan had been made or the service rendered to the government. It may seem wise to us that Hamilton did not attempt to solve the difficult questions which would have been involved in such readjustments of the debt, but according to Channing, probably nine-tenths of the congressmen expected, when they went to the first meeting of Congress, that there would be some sort of revision or scaling down of the debt.[24] The degree of inflation which had existed during most of the Revolutionary period, the fantastic prices which the government had frequently been forced to pay for goods and services, had caused many to suppose that the government would adopt some arbitrary ratio of old debts to new securities, rather than promise to pay in good money a debt that had been accumulated largely in terms of depreciated Continentals. There appears, however, to have been little question among members of the House as to the desirability of paying the face value of each security presented. The only important question raised was who should be paid.

The only modification of Hamilton's plan of funding which was seriously debated was that some attempt be made to discriminate between the original holders and the speculators who had purchased securities from these holders, usually at a fraction of their value and frequently with information from members of the government that the debt was to be paid in full.[25] Madison, who had until this point been very close to Hamilton, took the position that there must be a discrimination between speculators and original holders, who were usually soldiers and their families or creditors who had furnished supplies and money at the time when the cause looked darkest. In a speech made on the public credit in February, 1790, he said:

A composition, then, is the only expedient that remains; let it be a liberal one in favor of the present holders, let them have the highest price which has

[24] Edward Channing, *A History of the United States,* 6 vols. (New York, 1905-32), IV, 69. This is a point of great interest and importance, and it is to be regretted that Channing did not indicate the evidence upon which he based his conclusion. The letters of William Bingham and Stephen Higginson ("Letters from Two Business Men to Alexander Hamilton on Federal Fiscal Policy, November, 1789," James Wettereau, ed., *Journal of Economic and Business History,* III [1930-31], 667-86, hereafter cited as "Letters from Two Business Men"), in which both men urge substantially the method of funding which Hamilton followed, would suggest that it was not generally taken for granted among moneyed men that such a plan would be adopted. There seems, however, to be very little definite evidence as to the sort of arrangement which had been generally expected before Hamilton's plan was announced.

[25] See quotations from Andrew Craigie, in Davis, *American Corporations,* I, 188-89.

prevailed in the market; and let the residue belong to the original sufferers. This will not do perfect justice; but it will do more real justice, and perform more of the public faith, than any other expedient proposed.[26]

Hamilton had declared that the national credit was of one piece, that if the smallest part of it suffered injury or could be called into question, the whole was damaged;[27] and Madison's scheme of discrimination was treated in the House as though it were an effort to prevent the government from meeting its just obligations, even though the government would not have owed any less had discrimination been adopted. It was the representatives closest to Hamilton—Sedgwick and Ames of Massachusetts, Laurance of New York, Boudinot of New Jersey, and William L. Smith of South Carolina—who pushed the Funding Bill through in the form in which Hamilton wished it enacted. Their speeches, which were largely monotonous declamations on the nation's honor and which thus had little bearing upon the only important point raised, that of discrimination, probably did not affect the outcome; the twenty-nine members out of sixty-four who owned securities needed only four votes from the unorganized remainder of the House to pass the bill.[28]

In view of the charges made later against the Republicans, it is important that we should note that their opposition was not to the funding of the debt. They objected to the failure to discriminate between the original holders and the speculators. Likewise, the most serious objection of Madison and Jefferson to Assumption was to the details of the scheme, the manner in which the debt of the states was to be assumed, rather than to Assumption itself. The plan to establish the Bank was the first of Hamilton's measures which they met with unequivocal opposition. "Discrimination" justly describes the attitude they showed toward these earlier measures of his financial program.

The greatest opposition to the manner in which the debts were funded came from the Southern states[29] and from Pennsylvania. In those states

[26] Gaillard Hunt, ed., *The Writings of James Madison,* 9 vols. (New York, 1900-10), V, 444. Hereafter, Hunt, *Madison's Writings.*

[27] See "First Report on Public Credit," Lodge, *Hamilton's Works,* II, 227 ff.

[28] The yeas and nays were apparently not called on the Funding Bill, so it is impossible to know how the individual members voted.

[29] As strong a supporter of the Constitution as Henry Lee, then governor of Virginia, wrote to Madison from Berry Hill, Apr. 3, 1790, while the measures were before Congress, saying that he would rather "see the Union dissolve than submit to the rule of a fixed insolent northern majority." Gaillard Hunt, ed., *Disunion*

many who had been strongest in their support of the Constitution denounced the funding scheme in the strongest terms when it had become apparent that there was to be no attempt to discriminate between speculators and original holders. Benjamin Rush, who had been one of the strongest and most influential supporters of the national Constitution in Pennsylvania, believed shortly after the Funding Bill was passed that his state was very much opposed to it. "The Quakers & Germans who now govern directly or indirectly both our city and state, possess very few certificates; and we have more widows, orphans, and soldiers among us who have parted with their certificates than any city in the union." He felt, moreover, that Pennsylvania had been betrayed by those among her representatives who had supported Funding. He stated that both Clymer and Fitzsimmons, the most influential of the representatives from Pennsylvania in the first Congress, "left the city last fall determined on discrimination," but that the latter had now become "the midwife of a system every principle of which will be reprobated when established in our state."[30] Sedg-

---

Sentiment in Congress in 1794 (Washington, 1905), Introduction, 10. See also letter of Dr. Stuart to Washington concerning opposition in Virginia, Abingdon, Jun. 2, 1790, Worthington Chauncey Ford, ed., *The Writings of George Washington,* 14 vols. (New York and London, 1889-93), XI, 482-84 n; Edmund Randolph to Madison, Mar. 6, 1790, Madison Papers, LC; Madison to Monroe, Apr. 17, 1790, *ibid.;* Edmund Randolph to Madison, May 20, 1791, *ibid.;* Beverly Randolph to Madison, Jul. 12, 1791, *ibid.*

[30] Rush to Madison, Philadelphia, Apr. 10, 1790, Madison Papers, LC. The comments of Rush raise the question of how much of the debt remained in the hands of the original holders at the time it was funded, a point of the greatest significance if we are interested in the later political effects of Funding. Those who had had to part with their securities, particularly those whose securities had been bought by speculators who had been informed of the steps that were to be taken in regard to the debt, were probably among the most decided enemies of Hamilton and his later measures. Hamilton, in his "Vindication of the Funding System" (Lodge, *Hamilton's Works,* III, 20-21), states that in 1786-87, when New York State holders of Continental securities had an opportunity to trade them in for state securities on advantageous terms, "it appeared that about two-thirds of the debt remained in the hands of the original proprietors." He thought that alienation had been less in New England and Maryland than in New York, no greater in Pennsylvania and New Jersey, but that a more considerable alienation had taken place south of Maryland. Hamilton's estimate of the amount of alienation seems to be far smaller than that of anyone else who commented upon it at the time. R. J. Meigs wrote to Madison, Marietta, Feb. 1, 1792, that he thought that the old army had disposed of seven-eighths of its securities before announcement of redemption. Madison Papers, LC. Pelatiah Webster, who later favored discrimination between original holders and speculators, wrote in Jan., 1785, "It is a matter of public notoriety and general belief, that almost the *whole* of the *widows, orphans, soldiers,* and other *distressed public creditors,* have sold their

wick's account of the struggles he had with the Pennsylvania delegation, before he could bring them around to support these measures, bears out Rush's remark.[31]

In addition to the causes which Rush gave for Pennsylvania's opposition to Funding, there was the fact that Madison's suggestion for discrimination at no time received a fair hearing. The Pennsylvanians knew that it was not impossible to work out an equitable plan of discrimination between original and present holders, because they had done so with their own state debt. This plan of discrimination was at that time in operation. When Madison's similar proposal was denounced as impracticable, John Nicholson, who had worked out the details of the system of discrimination which was accepted by the Pennsylvania legislature, sent Madison a copy of this plan and said that it had been printed and was being dis-

---

securities, which are now in the hands of speculators, who are known to be very numerous, and many of whom have a vast amount of them." Quoted in Davis, *American Corporations,* I, 180-81. Noah Webster expressed similar sentiments in a letter of Mar. 5, 1787, to Governor James Bowdoin of Massachusetts, *ibid.,* 180 *n.* And in Jul., 1788, Andrew Craigie wrote, "The greater part of the public debt is held by rich people who can afford to keep their Interest." *Ibid.,* 181.

[31] Sedgwick to his wife, New York, Mar. 22, 1790. "The truth is we have not only to support our measures but we have also our party to keep in order. Without the delegation of Pennsylvania it is impossible to succeed. Mr. Fitzsimmons and Mr. Clymer the only men in it are but unexpectedly called home and how soon they will return is uncertain. Wadsworth, too, has thought it more to his interest to speculate than to attend to his duty in Congress and is gone home." Sedgwick Papers, Massachusetts Historical Society. Hereafter cited as Sedgwick Papers, MHS. Writing to his wife again on the state of the Assumption Bill, Apr. 13, 1790, Sedgwick said, "The event of assumption during the present session grows every day more and more uncertain. . . . Our great difficulty is with the delegation of Pennsylvania. They have no hesitation in declaring that they believe the assumption to be indispensable to the welfare of the country, but they seem to consider the measure as unpopular in that state and have not the firmness of spirit to give a decided preference to the welfare of the people over their own popularity." *Ibid.* Other evidence of sentiment in Pennsylvania against the funding scheme among those whom we should expect to be in favor of it is to be seen in the fact that a number of public creditors living in Pennsylvania who had petitioned Congress to take steps "for the revival of public credit and the advancement of the national honor" (see *Annals of Congress,* [Washington, 1834-56], Aug. 28, 1769) joined next year in a remonstrance against the Funding Act (see *Finance in American State Papers* [Washington, 1832-61], I, 76). The general opposition to Funding and Assumption throughout the South is well known, but little attention has been called to the similar feeling in Pennsylvania, though the opposition of the Pennsylvania public creditors is pointed out by Charles Franklin Dunbar in "Some Precedents Followed by Alexander Hamilton," *Quarterly Journal of Economics,* III (1888), 32-59.

tributed to the public.[32] The *Pennsylvania Gazette* ran a widely quoted
series of articles upon the effects that might be expected to follow Hamilton's method of funding:

Such injustice and oppression [as the funding scheme occasioned] may be
colored over with fine words, but there is a time coming when the pen of
history will detect and expose the folly of the arguments in favor of the proposed funding system as well as its iniquity. . . . If the balance still due the
army is paid them, it would spread money through every county and township of the United States, if paid to the speculator, all the cash of the United
States would soon center in our cities and later in England and Holland.

A few weeks later the same writer, *A Farmer,* stated that it would "be
impossible for farmers to borrow money to improve their lands, for who
will lend money to an individual for 6 per cent when government securities will yield from 8 to 12 per cent."

" 'The farmers,' he continues, 'never were in half the danger of being
ruined by the British government that they now are by their own.' "[33]

The evidences of opposition to the funding system throughout the
South, where the speculators had made their richest haul, are so numerous
that there is no need to labor the point. Similar feeling, so general in
Pennsylvania, was probably one of the strongest bonds in the future political unity between that state and the South. The opinion of the measure
held by those opposed to Funding, that it was rooted in calculated injustice, was strengthened by later developments. In 1795, when $1,181,000
was disbursed by the government on interest and capital payment on the
public debt, the four original New England states received $440,800 of
this amount. Massachusetts alone received much more than all the states
south of the Potomac; Connecticut, more than Virginia, North Carolina,
and Georgia combined.[34] The distribution of securities stirred up sectional
feeling, and the way in which money was raised to pay the debt caused

---

[32] Nicholson to Madison, Feb. 17, 1790. "The practicability of effecting a separate
provision for original holders, I am well convinced of. I have carried into effect a
similar plan in Penna. adopted by the legislature with respect to their *depreciation
debt* and with a few alterations it might be done with great exactness and very little
difficulty." Madison Papers, LC.

[33] Articles signed *A Farmer* in *Pennsylvania Gazette* (Philadelphia), Jan. 27,
Feb. 3, 1790. Quoted by Margaret Woodbury, *Public Opinion in Philadelphia, 1789-
1801,* in *Smith College Studies in History,* V (Oct., 1919-Jan., 1920), 45-46. Second
quotation in Miss Woodbury's words.

[34] See Charles Austin Beard, *An Economic Interpretation of the Constitution of
the United States* (New York, 1913), 36.

additional bitterness. Even in the late 1790's, Republican writers still found Funding a useful subject, and Joel Barlow, one of the most effective of them, wrote:

Besides the magnitude of our debt, the manner of funding it has had a pernicious influence on the policy of our government with foreign powers. The payment of the interest was made to depend in a great measure on the duties to be levied on imported merchandise, which were by law appropriated for fifteen years to this object. This made every stock-holder a partizan of our commercial connections with that country whose commerce with us was supposed principally to secure this revenue; however injurious those connections might become to the general interest of the United States. It is greatly owing to this unfortunate measure that our commerce has suffered so much during the present war from English and French depredations. For no one will deny that the latter were occasioned by our tame submission to the former.[35]

Popular feeling against Funding apparently died out quickly in the prosperity of the early 1790's, but later, when grievances against the Administration and the Federalist party became frequent, complaints of the evil effects of Funding were usually to be heard among them.

The funding system, which was the basis of Hamilton's whole financial program, did not arouse so much controversy as did the next step in the fulfillment of his plans, that by which the debts of all the states were to be assumed by the Federal government. A good deal of the opposition which Funding itself raised, as it was some time in coming to a head, vented itself on this second measure. Assumption was designed ostensibly to regulate the accounts between the debtor and the creditor states, but its other effects were so far-reaching that this must have seemed insignificant among them. It was like using a cannon to kill a mouse. If the national government was to pay the debts of the states,[36] it was obvious that the former would effectually dominate the revenue sources of the country, which under the Constitution were to be jointly tapped by state and Fed-

---

[35] Joel Barlow, Paris, Dec. 20, 1799, *Two Letters to the Citizens of the United States* (New Haven, 1806), 76-77.

[36] It is interesting to note that this measure was not undertaken as a result of petitions to Congress from state creditors that the national government assume the debts of the states. While the measure was under consideration some of the men who were most in favor of Assumption were terrified lest some of the state governments most in debt should undertake to provide completely for their creditors and thereby defeat Assumption.

eral governments. With this step taken, the individual states lost a large degree of their autonomy. Regarded from any point of view, Assumption meant a degree of consolidation and subordination of state to national authority which few had hitherto contemplated.

The general and uncritical shouldering by the new government of all claims against the Confederacy, which had been the distinguishing feature of the Funding Bill, had brought to the public view a debt of about 50 millions, and Assumption had added 22½ millions. Nearly 11 millions of this turned out to have been added unnecessarily, as Henry Adams shows.[37] The total debt of the government would have been around 60 millions, instead of over 70, if the precise nature of the account of each state with the old Confederacy had been ascertained before the debts were assumed. It was not generally known at the time how much the failure to investigate these circumstances was costing the government, but even without this knowledge the new total of the funded debt was sufficient to cause much anxiety. Apprehensive questions were asked by many who, on the whole, favored the measure: What interest would this debt bear? What proportion of the national revenue would be necessary to meet it? Could it ever be discharged? Questions such as these were asked. Other objections arose because of the way in which speculators had profited by buying up state securities; for their operations in the state funds, if not larger, were at least bolder than their operations in acquiring government securities. Many of these speculators were believed to live in New York and Massachusetts, states which would have profited greatly by having their debts assumed by the government even without this additional gain to their individual citizens. Virginia and Pennsylvania were discharging their debts satisfactorily, and their opposition to the measure formed a bond which later events were to strengthen. South Carolina alone of the Southern states was a large gainer by Assumption, and had it not been for the support of her members, Assumption would have had no chance from the beginning.[38] The immediate advantages or disadvantages for their individual states appear to have been uppermost in men's minds in their calculations upon this subject. Its larger implications and more

---

[37] Henry Adams, *The Life of Albert Gallatin* (Philadelphia and London, 1880), 168.

[38] See Madison to Edmund Pendleton, New York, Mar. 4, 1790, *Letters and Other Writings of James Madison,* 4 vols. (Congress Edition, Philadelphia, 1865), I, 508-9 (hereafter cited as Madison, *Letters*), for an account of the way in which particularly Massachusetts and South Carolina would profit from Assumption.

important consequences were to be revealed little by little over a period of some years.

The striking fact which has been generally ignored in the contest over Assumption is that the strongest opposition both inside the House and out came from men who had been most active in their support of the Constitution. Indeed, there were probably not more than half a dozen men in the first House of Representatives who had opposed the Constitution, Burke of South Carolina, Bloodworth of North Carolina, Bland and Griffin of Virginia, Heister of Pennsylvania, and Gerry of Massachusetts being the only members who had played prominent parts in the struggle against it. Of these six men three, Burke, Bland,[39] and Gerry, supported Assumption. On the other hand, Gilman and Livermore of New Hampshire; Hartley, Muhlenberg, and Scott of Pennsylvania; Madison and most of the rest of the Virginia delegation; all of the North Carolina delegation except Bloodworth; and Abraham Baldwin, Matthews, and Jackson of Georgia were active supporters of the Constitution, yet they opposed Assumption to the finish. We cannot discover whether the three New York members who voted against Assumption supported the Constitution or not. From what we do know about them it would seem probable that all three, Floyd, Hathorn, and Van Rensselaer, supported the Constitution. Perhaps the most striking fact in the whole effort to get Assumption accepted is that the four members of the House from Maryland and Virginia who changed their votes on Assumption after the famous dinner at which Jefferson and Hamilton discussed the subject with them had all been supporters of the Constitution.[40]

The line which is asserted by some to run from the supporters of the Constitution to the Federalist party and from its opponents to the Republican was broken on this occasion, and with these basic measures of Hamilton's financial program a new principle of division appeared in national politics. At the Constitutional Convention the basic division which appeared had not been sectional, but between the large and the small states. Once the

[39] See *Annals of Congress*, Jul. 24, 1790. Bland was not present at the final vote on Assumption, but he was in favor of the measure. He wrote to Patrick Henry, Mar. 9, 1790, "that having sworn to support the constitution he was voting for every measure of energy and consolidation; that government once assumed over so extensive a dominion must fall into anarchy or be supported with vigor." Hunt, *Madison's Writings*, VI, 8 *n*. (Hunt's wording.)

[40] For evidence that Richard Bland Lee and Alexander White of Virginia, Daniel Carroll and George Gale of Maryland, were the four men whose votes were changed, see Richard Henry Lee to William Lee, New York, Jul. 27, 1790, James Curtis Ballagh, ed., *The Letters of Richard Henry Lee*, 2 vols. (New York, 1911-14), II, 535.

great compromise of the Constitution was made, by which each state was represented in the Senate by two men and in the House according to population, there was no longer any ground for a conflict of interest between the large and small states. The former basis of division, which it had been feared would make any union impossible, did not appear in Congress; and until the first measures of Hamilton's financial program were proposed, there did not seem to be any recurring basis of division among the members of the House of Representatives. Of the first session of Congress, before the proposal of any of the measures of Hamilton's program, Madison wrote:

In general, the interests and ideas of the Northern and Southern States have been less adverse than was predicted by the opponents or hoped by the friends of the new Government. Members from the same State, or the same part of the Union, are as often separated on questions from each other as they are united in opposition to other States or other quarters of the Continent.[41]

The atmosphere of harmony was not restricted to the House of Representatives but was apparent everywhere, even among those who had opposed the adoption of the Constitution. Madison wrote to Washington in November, 1789:

As far as I can gather, the great bulk of the late opponents are entirely at rest, and more likely to censure a further opposition to the Government, as now administered, than the Government itself. One of the principal leaders of the Baptists lately sent me word that the amendments had entirely satisfied the disaffected of his sect, and that it would appear in their subsequent conduct.[42]

And William Bingham wrote to Hamilton only a few days later, "The present Period is very favorable for carrying into Effect a System of Taxation, as the Affection of the People are so rivetted to the New Government, that their minds will be easily conciliated to all its operations."[43]

All the evidence would indicate that the second session of the first Congress, to which the Funding and Assumption Bills were presented, found the people of the whole country extraordinarily united in support of the new government.[44] They realized that this was perhaps their last chance

[41] Madison to Jefferson, New York, May 9, 1789, Madison, *Letters,* I, 466.
[42] Madison to Washington, Orange, Nov. 20, 1789, *ibid.,* 496.
[43] "Letters of Two Business Men," 679.
[44] For evidence of widespread approval of the Constitution at the time of its adoption in Portsmouth, New Hampshire, and Boston, places where there had been

to obliterate the pettiness and selfishness of the past few years, the full dangers of which seem to have become apparent only as the people rose above themselves and experienced a new union and harmony.

This spirit of union and harmony was shattered, both inside the House of Representatives and among the public at large, by the measures of Hamilton's financial program. A sharp sectional division appeared in the voting upon the measures of that program, a division which foreshadowed the first phase in the growth of national parties. There were two votes against Assumption from New Hampshire but none from the other New England states. There were three votes against it from New York, none against it from New Jersey, and four against it from Pennsylvania. Thus from the Northern states there were nine votes against the measure, while there were twenty-four in favor of it. In the South there were for Assumption one vote from Delaware, two from Maryland, two from Virginia, and five from South Carolina.[45] These make a total of ten for the bill, while eighteen were against it, but we should remember that the four votes from Maryland and Virginia had to be arranged, and that South Carolina was by no means so Federalist upon other measures as upon this. On the Excise Bill there were but two votes in opposition in New York and the states to the north. There were four votes against it from Pennsylvania, making a total from the Northern states of six against the bill, while twenty-eight were for it. In the South there were one vote for the bill from Delaware, one from Maryland, four from Virginia, and one from South Carolina, which made a total of seven for the measure, and there were fifteen against it from the representatives of that section.[46] On the bill to establish the Bank there was but one vote in opposition from the Northern states, that of Grout of Massachusetts, making the total of those states thirty-three to one. The vote of the Southern states on this measure was six for it, nineteen against it.[47] Nothing like this sectional division had been seen in the voting before these measures were introduced.

It cannot be assumed, however, that the strong support which New England representatives gave Hamilton's measures in the House reflected the sentiment of their section accurately. There is ample evidence from the

much opposition and where the Republicans were to be strong, see Lawrence Shaw Mayo, *John Langdon of New Hampshire* (Concord, New Hampshire, 1937), 216-21, and John C. Miller, *Sam Adams, Pioneer in Propaganda* (Boston, 1936), 384.

[45] *Annals of Congress*, Jul. 26, 1790.
[46] *Ibid.*, Jan. 27, 1791.
[47] *Ibid.*, Feb. 8, 1791.

best Federalist sources[48] that even in the most conservative circles of New England there was much doubt as to the wisdom of Assumption and a good deal of opposition to it. Nothing could show the scope and audacity of Hamilton's economic program as it appeared to his contemporaries so well as the fact that many members of the groups who were supposed to benefit most from Assumption feared that here Hamilton was going much too fast. According to Samuel Henshaw, Stephen Higginson "liked the plan generally, but was fearful that it was too rigid, prompt and energetic for this early period of our national existence."[49] Gouverneur Morris thought that Hamilton was not only going too fast, but in the wrong direction as well. He wrote from London when he heard that Assumption had been suggested, "To assume the payment of what the States owe, merely because they owe it, seems to my capacity not more rational, than to assume the debts of corporations, or of individuals." Later in this letter he said, "If the individual or community be in debt, or not in debt, to others, is a circumstance which the public, the Union, America, in short, has nothing to do with."[50]

Gouverneur Morris's letter shows that other Federalists than those from New England were opposed to Assumption when it was proposed, but the strongest protests against it from those who were to remain loyal Federalists appear to have come from Massachusetts. The prevalence of opposition in conservative circles there raises the question of how the measure got the

[48] John Quincy Adams to John Adams, Newburyport, Mar. 19, 1790, Worthington Chauncey Ford, ed., *The Writings of John Quincy Adams,* 7 vols. (New York, 1913-17), I, 48; same to same, Newburyport, April 5, 1790, *ibid.,* 50; Christopher Gore to Rufus King, Boston, Jan. 24, 1790, Charles R. King, ed., *The Life and Correspondence of Rufus King,* 6 vols. (New York, 1894-1900), I, 385 (hereafter cited as King, *Correspondence*); same to same, Boston, May 30, 1790, *ibid.,* 388; Nathaniel Gorham to Sedgwick, Jan. 12, 1790, Sedgwick Papers, MHS; same to same, Jan. 23, 1790, *ibid.;* Henshaw to Sedgwick, Boston, Jan. 27, 1790, *ibid.;* same to same, Boston, Jan. 30, 1790, *ibid.* Two letters from Henry Van Schaack to Sedgwick, Pittsfield, May 3, 1794, and Feb. 13, 1797, indicate that Assumption continued to be used by the opposition in their attacks on the Administration and that the Federalists were not able to meet all their arguments. In the first of these letters Van Schaack urges Sedgwick to get an abstract from the Treasury books to give him additional information to refute skeptics. The second letter suggests that he had been reading Gallatin's "A Sketch of the Finances of the United States" (Henry Adams, ed., *The Writings of Albert Gallatin* 3 vols. [Philadelphia, 1879], III, 69-207; hereafter cited as Gallatin, *Writings*) and that he had been partially convinced, for the time, by it. *Ibid.*

[49] Henshaw to Sedgwick, Boston, Feb. 14, 1790, *ibid.*

[50] Gouverneur Morris to Robert Morris, London, Jul. 31, 1790, Jared Sparks. ed., *Life of Gouverneur Morris with Selections from His Correspondence and Miscellaneous Papers,* 3 vols. (Boston, 1832), III, 11-13. Hereafter, Sparks, *Life of G. Morris.*

unanimous vote of the Massachusetts members. At least a part of the answer lies in the exertions of Theodore Sedgwick, the most strenuous of Hamilton's supporters in the first Congress. One of his own letters gives the following account of the methods by which Assumption was put through: "During the passage of the assumption bill we had several hairbreadth escapes from ruin. My colleague Gerry, who is the veriest quiddle in nature, would be frequently seduced by the enemy." A motion had been offered excluding all notes not presented by the original holders unless the owner would swear that he had not purchased between certain dates. "This was a kind of self-denying purgation ordinance designed to declare the purity of the members, and was therefore precisely of a nature to operate on his mind." Gerry was in favor of this bill, and Sedgwick labored with him privately to give it up, "telling him it was supported by insidious men," but Gerry was not convinced. "I was finally obliged to get up in the House and tell him what I had so often before said to him, and concluded by declaring that if he persisted he should stand responsible to Massachusetts for the failure of this measure so beneficial to our constituents. This had its effect and to his utter disgrace he was obliged to abandon his object."[51] This letter from Sedgwick shows the part that Hamilton's intimate associates in Congress played in getting his favorite measures adopted, a part which was frequently quite as important as that ascribed to them by their opponents.

We have been concerned with the immediate repercussions of Hamilton's program, both in the House and among the more well-informed of the general public, rather than with its long-run effects upon the growth of parties. But it should be apparent that a measure which so seriously alarmed many of those from the section which it benefited most, a measure which was later found to have increased the debt unnecessarily and to have led to a more scandalous use of official influence and information for the benefit of speculators than even the Funding Bill, contained ample ammunition for the party battle which was soon to break out. The threats of disunion if the bill were not passed and such coercion as Sedgwick applied to Gerry on the floor of the House showed an eagerness for the passing of this measure which was to cause more bitterness later than at the time.

If we view Hamilton's program for a moment in its relation to the

[51] Sedgwick to Ephraim Williams, Philadelphia, Jan. 31, 1793, Sedgwick Papers, MHS.

later growth of political parties, we are struck by a curious circumstance. The basic measures of his plan, Funding and Assumption, have been treated by historians and economists in almost every respect except that of their effect on public opinion. On the other hand, the effects on public opinion of two less important measures, the establishment of the Bank and of the excise system, are frequently remarked upon. The former had immediate effects in dividing opinion by producing the first complete expositions of the opposing views of the Constitution which were to become the official creeds of the two parties; the latter had its effect by bringing about the Whiskey Rebellion. These later measures came at a time when party division was already well on its way, and they have tended to obscure the effects of Funding and Assumption. The greater importance of the earlier measures is due to the fact that so much of later Federalist policy grows out of them. It is in studying these policies, which so frequently went directly in the face of the main currents of opinion, that we shall find the first milestones in the growth of parties.

Perhaps the most important single effect, as far as the growth of parties is concerned, of the establishment of the Bank and the setting up of the Excise was that these measures, instead of redressing the balance between sections and interests which many thought had been so disturbed by Hamilton's first measures, gave additional advantages to New England and the moneyed group. They brought no solace to the sections and groups most outraged by Funding and Assumption. In New England only the large distillers of West Indian molasses were affected by the Excise, and they had already been placated by favorable concessions in the duty paid on both foreign liquors and those made in this country from foreign materials. Large areas of the South and of western Pennsylvania, however, found little comfort in any of the provisions of the Excise on whiskey, particularly after the provision exempting stills of less than fifty-gallon capacity was removed in 1792. The smallest details of the excise system seemed designed to work hardship, since almost all those accused under it had to make long journeys for trial; and as soon as it became apparent that no attention was to be paid to the numerous petitions to have the Excise Bill changed or withdrawn, it was evaded and defied. Thus in the last parts of Hamilton's program, where he could have afforded concessions which might have alleviated some of the bitterness caused by his fundamental measures, he passed by the opportunity and extended the privileges of the few and the burdens of the many which were implied in its framework.

Having examined Hamilton's program in its relation to public opinion and the later growth of parties, we turn to the economic reasoning by which Hamilton supported the various parts of his program. "In the 'Vindication of Funding' . . . he . . . adds that if a government borrows a hundred dollars, it spends it, and that is capital; while the bond may be sold, and is another. Thus the credit of government produces a new capital of a hundred dollars."[52] Sumner says of this reasoning, "These notions show a remarkable amount of confusion in regard to money, capital, and debt, in the mind of a man who has a great reputation as a financier."[53] And of the reasoning by which Hamilton defended Assumption, Sumner says, ". . . although it was creditable to his sense of justice, [it] is not strong when regarded from the political point of view. It remained true that he was reaching out for a duty which did not necessarily devolve upon him, and was exposing the Federal Government to a new trial, when he thought he was winning strength for it."[54]

Concerning Hamilton's arguments for a close connection between the Bank and the government, Sumner writes:

There was no need, in the case of the Bank of the United States, of allowing subscriptions in the public debt. The public debt was all provided for independently of the bank. . . . The government of the United States never realized any gain whatever from this device. The expectation was unfounded and illusory, and the opposition were justified in saying that if it had been real, it would have been derogatory to the government.

Another very great vice in Hamilton's bank was the arrangement by which the United States government, being itself at the time impecunious, subscribed stock in the bank and gave its notes for the subscription.[55]

Sumner sees in this precedent the rise of the most vicious practices of government finance, which did not come to an end until the establishment of the independent sub-treasury system. Elsewhere he states, "In these passages [from the letters, newspaper articles, and the Federalist reports on public credit and on the national bank] we see that he was under the dominion of the most vicious fallacies with regard to money and banking, and that his idea of a bank did not go beyond some of the vulgar misconceptions about it."[56]

In his famous letter to John Sullivan in 1780, urging the establishment

[52] Sumner, *Alexander Hamilton*, 150.
[53] *Ibid.*   [54] *Ibid.*, 157.   [55] *Ibid.*, 164.   [56] *Ibid.*, 167.

of a national bank, Hamilton stated that this country was then in the same condition as France before Law's Mississippi scheme: "The foundation [of that scheme] was good, but the superstructure too vast"; and that we should select the good in this and other plans, "avoiding the defects and excesses. Something on a similar principle in America will alone accomplish the restoration of paper credit. . . ."[57] He seems even in later years to have maintained the attitude toward government finance which is revealed in this statement.

Oliver Wolcott, one of Hamilton's closest disciples, was appalled at the financial condition of the national government when he succeeded Hamilton as Secretary of the Treasury. In September, 1795, he wrote to Hamilton saying that public affairs were in a critical state and that he did not see how the affairs of the Treasury were to be managed:

Our foreign resources are dried up; our domestic are deeply anticipated, at least as respects the bank. Banks are multiplying like mushrooms. The prices of all our exports are impaired by paper negotiations and unfounded projects, so that no foreign market will indemnify the shippers. Our commerce is harrassed by the war, and our internal revenue unproductive of the expected sums, owing to prejudice, combination, and the want of competent officers. Usury absorbs much of that capital which might be calculated upon as a resource, if visionary speculations could be destroyed.[58]

Hamilton seemed unconcerned by this grave financial situation and answered Wolcott, "The worst evil we can struggle with, is inefficiency in the measures of government."[59] At the time of Fries' Rebellion he put what seems to have been his idea at this time even more clearly: "The consideration of expense is of no moment compared with the advantages of energy."[60]

Hamilton's financial program and his later policies are usually defended as having been indispensable, not because they contributed energy to the government, but because they were the embodiment of sound finance. Hamilton is pictured ordinarily as a man of profound insight into the principles of economics and finance, who was content to let the chips fall

[57] Lodge, Hamilton's Works, III, 332-33. (On p. 319 Lodge mistakenly describes this letter as written to Robert Morris.)

[58] Wolcott to Hamilton, Philadelphia, Sept. 26, 1795, Hamilton, Hamilton's Works, VI, 39-40.

[59] Hamilton to Wolcott, New York, Oct. 3, 1795, ibid., 40.

[60] Hamilton to McHenry, New York, Mar. 18, 1799, Lodge, Hamilton's Works, VII, 69.

where they might. If his policies cannot be defended by this reasoning, if his economic tenets and reasoning were defective, or if he was inclined to subordinate financial policy to other purposes, we should see what the objects were that he sought to gain. If the energy which they imparted to the government is to be the criterion for judging his financial measures, we should inquire into what he meant by energy.

Oliver Wolcott, as Hamilton's assistant in the Treasury Department, wrote a letter to his father about the time that Assumption was first presented to the House of Representatives, which is frequently considered as expressing Hamilton's purposes at this time:

I can consider a funding system as important, in no other way than as an engine of government. The only question is what the engine shall be. The influence of a clergy, nobility and armies, are and ought to be out of the question in this country; but unless some active principle of the human mind can be interested in support of the government, no civil establishments can be formed, which will not appear like useless and expensive pageants, and by their unpopularity weaken the government which they are intended to support. . . .

For these reasons I think the State debts ought to be assumed, as without the assumption the political purposes which I have enumerated, cannot be attained. This will indeed increase the debt in the United States, to a degree which will be very inconvenient. The taxes necessary to pay the interest will be burdensome, and they will appear to be just, only to those who believe that the good attained is more important than the evil which is suffered.[61]

The reasoning sounds like that of Hamilton; his other statements that it was necessary to have propertied men financially interested in the new government[62] would seem ample warrant for the assumption that Wolcott has given here a faithful paraphrase of Hamilton's purposes as expressed in his economic program. When we look at Hamilton's first measures in this light, instead of thinking of them as having been the sole means of saving national credit, their fitness for their real purpose is evident, and it is only then that the artistic economy with which they were fashioned can

[61] Oliver Wolcott to Oliver Wolcott, Sr., New York, Mar. 27, 1790, Gibbs, *Memoirs*, I, 43.

[62] Hamilton to Sullivan, 1780 (only date given): "The only plan that can preserve the currency is one that will make it the *immediate* interest of the moneyed men to co-operate with government in its support." Lodge, *Hamilton's Works*, III, 332.

be justly appreciated. If Hamilton's method of applying Funding and Assumption raised the debt to a higher total than the establishing of national credit would have required, it may also have given an opportunity to interest that many more moneyed men in the new government. By refusing to discriminate between original holders and speculators, he secured for the latter their great profits. From any point of view, a more perfect device for the concentration of wealth at that time could hardly have been conceived. As Rexford Tugwell and Joseph Dorfman put it:

The reports of Hamilton in 1790 and 1791, taken together, constitute a theoretical plan which is just beginning to be appreciated. The economic organization logically involved was grand and imperial in scope. A fully negotiable funded debt, drained originally from the small-property classes and met by taxes paid by the masses, was to be used by an emerging moneyed class to create profitable speculative enterprises in lands, industry, and finance.[63]

From the point of view of the interest of the country as a whole, the axioms upon which Hamilton's program rested may be false, the reasoning by which it was supported, defective or strained; but from the point of view of the creation and strengthening of a moneyed interest, his whole plan was flawless both in conception and execution.

The working out of Hamilton's economic program in the realm of practical politics, the specific relations between it and his later policies, and the effects of both on the development of parties, will be treated in the course of this study; but the question of his larger ends, his ultimate purposes as revealed in this system, may be profitably considered here. If this system was primarily "an engine of government," what sort of engine was it?

If we look at the career of Hamilton as a whole, a few dominant ideas, each of which would support the others in the circumstances of that time, are evident. Hamilton put his trust in the privileged classes and considered their interests as inseparable from those of society as a whole. He wanted a close collaboration between this country and England. He aimed at the closest possible union, even a high degree of consolidation, between the different parts of this country, and he wanted a powerful central government. These aims were so closely related in the conditions of the time

[63] Rexford Guy Tugwell and Joseph Dorfman, "Alexander Hamilton: Nation-maker," *Columbia University Quarterly* (XXIX and XXX, 1937 and 1938), XXX, 63-4.

that they are perhaps aspects of the same plan, and he probably thought of them as different means toward a single goal. The economic program which he advanced furthered these aims in every respect. It made for the supremacy of the propertied classes; it involved as much consolidation and as great a centralization of power as would have been accepted at that time; and it brought in its train intimate commercial and diplomatic relations with Great Britain. All Hamilton's fundamental views are implied in this program, and it is here that we see them most closely integrated.

Sumner states that those parts of Hamilton's system which were not necessary for the financial integrity of the new government were incorporated because of "political expediency,"[64] but this pale term is inadequate to explain the passionate conviction with which Hamilton defended his whole scheme, his fear that if a single part of it were not adopted or were abandoned, the whole would be weakened.[65] This devotion to his system sprang from his conception of what society should be, and his knowledge that the whole of the system was necessary before the special interests of the moneyed group could be so enmeshed in those of the general public that it would be impossible for anyone to attack the former without laying himself open to the charge that it was in reality the latter against which he was laying stealthy designs. Hamilton was incidentally strengthening and consolidating interests friendly to his policies which would be powerful in Congress, but he was primarily concerned with putting the nation on the path he thought it should follow.

The questions of who supported Hamilton's financial program and why they did so are perhaps as important in a study of the formation of parties as is any analysis of Hamilton's purposes in urging this program. The passing of his basic measures has sometimes been attributed to the greed of speculating congressmen and the influence of other speculators. Yet the fact that many congressmen did hold government and state securi-

[64] ". . . assumption stood upon a very different footing [from funding]. It was a matter of political expediency, not of simple financial rectitude; and its expediency remains in doubt to this day." Sumner, *Alexander Hamilton*, 154.

[65] In the spring of 1796 a bill was moved in Congress which would have authorized the sale of bank stock owned by the government, the proceeds to be used to pay off a sum due from the government to the bank. Hamilton wrote to Wolcott, May 30, 1796, "I perceive Congress are invading the Sinking Fund System. If this goes through, and is sanctioned by the President, the fabric of public credit is prostrate, and the country and the President are disgraced. Treasury bills and every expedient, however costly, to meet exigencies, must be preferable in the event to such an overthrow of system." Hamilton Papers, LC.

ties, the values of which were greatly increased by Funding and Assumption, is no proof that they were speculators, or that they had made use of official information to acquire securities which they knew would be affected by measures pending. Within little more than a year after the passing of Funding and Assumption, the Republicans began to charge that Federalist congressmen had made precisely this use of their official positions, but in the absence of better evidence than the Republicans were able to present in support of these charges, they were labeled as those of men so hostile to the new government that they would go to any length in an attempt to discredit it.

The question whether or not congressmen were speculators and not merely security holders was not cleared up at the time, but a letter of Andrew Craigie offers conclusive evidence that a number of congressmen did make use of their official positions to aid their speculations in government securities in 1789 and 1790. Craigie states in this letter that the consideration of the government debt was delayed until these men could get their affairs in shape to reap the greatest possible benefit from the new measures. Craigie was a Boston speculator who, during much of the time that the first Congress was in session, stayed in New York in a boarding house with six New England congressmen, numbering among them Hamilton's strongest supporters. In January, 1790, while Congress was beginning its considerations of Hamilton's first report, Christopher Gore, also deep in speculation, said of Craigie, "Should a bill of sale be given of Congress, Andrew surely would pass as appurtenant,"[66] and perhaps no better authority than Craigie's could be found for the statement which he made on the speculations of congressmen to one of his associates in September, 1789. He wrote that Congress would not deal with the debt until after the recess for several reasons, among which he included the following: "Besides there are many who are interested in delaying the Business either because they have borrowed large sums of the debt which they have to purchase or because their private arrangements are not in readiness for speculation."[67]

The fact that congressmen were speculating in the government funds and that such large speculators as Craigie and William Duer were in a position to know the inmost secrets of Congress and the Treasury is

[66] Remark quoted from Christopher Gore by Bassinger Foster, Jr., in letter to Craigie, Boston, Jan. 15, 1790, Craigie Papers, Vol. I, American Antiquarian Society, Worcester.

[67] Craigie to Daniel Parker, *ibid.,* Box III, Miscellaneous.

important as showing that there was a basis of fact for later Republican charges, but it does not serve to explain clearly the basis of party division; for neither of the first national political parties deserves to be judged by or identified with its camp followers. The Federalist party, particularly in these years, rested upon a much broader base than that offered by speculators. The passing of Hamilton's program can be attributed to interested speculators and their associates in Congress in only a superficial sense. According to later Republican charges, the honest, disinterested congressmen were divided fairly evenly on many of Hamilton's measures, the balance being turned by those who were in a position to profit directly, as was the case with the members who had bought state securities in the expectation that Assumption would be adopted. Thus even by the later admission of Hamilton's opponents, who were only too prone to identify Federalism and speculation, there were many in Congress who supported his measures without any prospect of profiting from them except as they promised to benefit the country as a whole. It is by directing our attention to supporters of this sort that we shall get the greatest light on the relation of Hamilton's measures to the process of party formation.

The men who supported Hamilton's program from a motive other than direct personal gain may be roughly divided into those who remained Federalists and those who finally went over to the opposition though they had supported Hamilton's early measures. The first group was made up of men who, though they might think specific measures unwise, welcomed the larger implications of Hamilton's financial program as well as those of his later policy, as they became increasingly clear to them. As these men saw them, Hamilton's measures were designed to restore control to the conservatives without openly challenging the current popular dogmas of government. Hamilton would have yielded the battle as far as declamation and political theory were concerned, lest his commanding position on a more decisive field be endangered. With the promulgation of his program, the more astute conservatives realized that they had found a daring and resourceful leader. There were groups in every state who had opposed any change in the relation of classes during and since the Revolution, to whom that movement meant primarily the preservation of the social structure of colonial times with themselves occupying the first, rather than the second or third, places; and the leaders of such groups were not slow to grasp the implications of Hamilton's program. Gouverneur Morris once remarked to John Jay, "Finance, my friend, all that is left of the American Revolution grounds there,"[68] and if he was thinking of the American Revolution as a social movement, this remark might well serve as the motto of Hamilton's economic program. Those who wanted the preservation of an old-world society with the additional advantage of exploiting a new continent could not have done better than to give Hamilton their undivided allegiance. He merited Talleyrand's tribute: "Il avait deviné l'Europe."[69]

It should be noted, however, that all conservatives in the United States are not to be identified too closely, nor for too long a period, with Hamilton's supporters. Some men of very conservative views who had upheld his early measures later joined his opponents when they became convinced that they had been deceived in his purposes. Such men as John Dickinson, John Langdon, George Wythe, and Charles Pinckney, conservative leaders in their respective states in 1789, had gone over to the opposition by 1796. Others, like Rush and Madison, equally strong supporters of the Constitution, were alienated by Hamilton's earlier measures. A consideration of the political affiliations of the most prominent men in the country from 1789 to the end of the decade shows that from the time of Hamilton's first measures there was much shifting from one party to the other.

The effect of Hamilton's measures upon those who, though hostile to Hamilton, remained in the Federalist party should also be considered. John Adams, who hated banks,[70] the moneyed interest, and in fact Hamil-

---

[68] Lodge, *Hamilton's Works,* II, 289 is one of several places where this remark is quoted without any reference to the date or the circumstances in which it was made. There is, therefore, no evidence that Morris had Hamilton's program in mind when he made this statement.

[69] Gertrude Franklin Atherton, *The Conqueror: Being the True and Romantic Story of Alexander Hamilton* (New York, 1916), quoted on title page.

[70] Adams to Benjamin Rush, Quincy, Aug. 28, 1811. "Funds and banks I never approved, or was satisfied with our funding system; it was founded on no consistent principle; it was contrived to enrich particular individuals at the public expense. Our whole banking system I ever abhorred, I continue to abhor, and shall die abhorring."

He continues later in the same letter, "A national bank of deposit I believe to be wise, just, prudent, economical, and necessary. But every bank of discount, every bank by which interest is to be paid or profit of any kind made by the deponent, is downright corruption. It is taxing the public for the benefit and profit of the individuals; it is worse than old tenor, continental currency, or any other paper money." Charles Francis Adams, ed., *The Life and Works of John Adams,* 10 vols. (Boston, 1850-56), IX, 638. Hereafter cited as Adams, *Works.* And in a letter to John Taylor of Caroline, Quincy, Mar. 12, 1819, Adams wrote, "I have never had but one opinion concerning banking, from the institution of the first, in Philadelphia, by Mr. Robert Morris and Mr. Gouverneur Morris, and that opinion has uniformly been that the banks have done more injury to the religion, morality, tranquillity, prosperity, and

ton's whole conception of the basis of government, supported his early measures although he distrusted them. In supporting measures which he did not like but which seemed to him necessary for the success of the new government, Adams probably represented more accurately than Hamilton ever did the views of the rank and file of those who remained Federalist, but a crusty personality and a mass of abstruse political theory such as his were not designed to bring public sentiment to a focus, no matter how strong it was potentially. Since he could not make an articulate political force of those whose views he represented, the solid, homely, and indigenous aspects of Federalism were largely obscured, and Hamilton's party leadership was not challenged until the party split in 1799. Hamilton's policy divided his erstwhile supporters while it united his opponents, and the true measure of his importance in the formation of political parties can be judged only by following both the growth of the Republicans and the disintegration of the Federalists. It may be noted in passing that since Hamilton's measures did not preserve the degree of unity which the conservatives had attained in 1789, efforts to treat the political division of the 1790's in strictly economic terms are likely to be highly misleading.

It is customary to contrast Hamilton's views of society with his own humble and uncertain origins on a small West Indian island, but any reflection upon the highly centralized economic control, the hierarchies of the caste system, and the dependent position of these sugar islands in the mercantile scheme should serve to explain Hamilton's vision of the perfect state. We can see in the purposes of his mature years the perfect, if inverted, reflection of the circumstances and vicissitudes of his youth. More than most men, Hamilton deserves to be discussed in terms of his purpose as a whole. Instead of following this procedure, however, both those who attack and those who defend him are likely to concentrate on the personal aspects of his policies, upon his motives, instead of judging the whole as a policy of creative statesmanship.

The great reliance of Hamilton's defenders has been upon his personal honesty and unselfish devotion to the United States, the assumption being that as long as we grant him these qualities, his policies were not open to attack. Both defense and criticism of him have echoed the partisan language of the 1790's, and both have been equally beside the point which

---

even wealth of the nation, than they can have done or ever will do good. They are like party spirit, the delusion of the many for the interest of a few." *Ibid.*, X, 375.

is of primary significance for us. He himself construed attacks upon his system as efforts to convict him of personal dishonesty, and he defended all his measures, particularly to Washington, from the impregnable fortress of his personal honor; but if we wish to see how his program divided public opinion at the time, we merely cloud the issue by entering into the question of his own integrity and disinterestedness. His political enemies would have had a powerful weapon if they could have shown that he profited personally from policies that they wished to have overthrown, but that is the only importance, as far as the history of the country is concerned, of the question of Hamilton's personal character. Hamilton honest was a much more powerful adversary than Hamilton as an interested speculator, and a conspicuous integrity was indispensable for the part that he wished to play in the new government. This fact does not mean that he had to restrain a desire for personal enrichment lest it conflict with his other aims. He cared little for money either as a citizen or a statesman;[71] he saw it only as a means. A man can have only one dominating urge, and Hamilton's was for power and influence. He did not need money for his own purposes as long as he had the support of those who had money. Again we go wandering off into the labyrinth of the merely personal if we are too concerned as to whether Hamilton's desire for power was selfish, or whether he only wanted a government which was the embodiment of power and thought his measures the best way of attaining it. We may grant every contention of his admirers in support of the latter thesis and still see that such a single-minded pursuit of power terminates either in revolt and disunion or in the Leviathan state. Though primarily concerned with the creation of a powerful state, Hamilton seems never to have asked himself how powerful a state could be if it were not based on the loyalty, affections, and best interests of all of its citizens.

[71] Of the personal affairs of Hamilton at the time of his death Gouverneur Morris wrote to Robert Morris, Morrisania, Jul. 20, 1804, "His affairs are sadly deranged. He has made a considerable purchase of land in no very eligible situation and of a quality inferior to some which is now on the market. After paying and binding himself to pay he found a heavy mortgage which he was obliged to take up and of course to encumber himself still more. His country house has according to custom cost him much more than he thought it would." Morris concluded that under the best of circumstances Hamilton would have been several years clearing off these encumbrances. (Letterbooks of Gouverneur Morris, Library of Congress.) Thus there were other reasons in addition to Hamilton's personal honesty which caused him to die poor.

3. GEORGE WASHINGTON

If we ask how Hamilton attained and kept the influence which he had from 1789 to 1801, the answer is that it was primarily because of his standing with Washington. Such an answer does not call into question the genius and magnetism of Hamilton, nor his single-minded devotion to the interest of the country as he saw it. His extraordinary endowments, however, were so frequently devoted to purposes which were contrary to tradition and popular feeling that his possession of them does not account for the almost incredible influence which remained at his command until after the election of 1800. In his dissertation, *Some Presidential Interpretations of the Presidency,* Norman Small describes Hamilton's customary procedure in getting his measures put into effect in the following terms:

. . . by shielding his political maneuvres behind the cloak of the President's reputation, Hamilton not only carried out his program with little interference, but practically deprived his opponents of a means of protest; for the latter refused to risk popular condemnation by an attack which, though directed against the Secretary, would have unavoidably included the President. Thus proceeding boldly in pursuit of his policies Hamilton submitted reports to Congress, expounding in detail both the reason why and the manner in which the financial recommendations contained in the President's messages should be adopted, saw to it that party associates in accord with his opinions were appointed to committees deliberating on his measures, and finally when a doubt arose as to the fate of his program, rounded up his political adherents in order to secure a majority vote in favor of his bills. In fact the conduct of the Federalists in Congress was invariably predetermined by the decisions reached in their own secret party meetings at which Hamilton presided.[72]

According to this view, Washington's recommendation of Hamilton's measures was not the only thing necessary to get these measures adopted, but it was the most essential. The President's approval, helpful in getting measures through Congress, also provided the best possible protection for them against popular criticism.

The influence of Washington himself, from the establishment of the new government to his death, is of an importance which all who have studied the period have acknowledged. Affection for him and complete trust in him were at times during this period probably the only sentiments

[72] Norman Jerome Small, *Some Presidential Interpretations of the Presidency* (Baltimore, 1932), 164.

which were shared without important reservations by the mass of the people throughout the country. These sentiments were called into service to support government policy at every important crisis from 1793 on, and provided on these occasions the most important check on criticism of the government's course.

There can be little doubt as to the effectiveness of Washington's influence; the questions arise when one begins to examine the relation of Washington himself to the use made of his influence. How much did he understand of the things being done in his name? How did those who made the greatest use of him actually regard him? Was he a responsible executive, making his own decisions after consulting his advisers, or was he something of a figurehead? Was he a sick, tired old man who went grimly through the ceremonies laid out for him, or was he an actual leader of his people, whose own deepest convictions and ultimate aims were expressed in the policies he was shaping?

A final answer to such questions as these can never be given; if the true answer were susceptible of discovery and proof, it could not be a simple one. Yet they are of the greatest importance for a study of this period, and whatever evidence we can find as to the nature of the influence which Washington exerted should be applied to them.

A legendary figure from the Revolution on, Washington reached the final stages of his apotheosis with the adoption of the Constitution and the establishment of the new government. Samuel Henshaw, writing to Sedgwick in June, 1789, about the deplorable character of the Massachusetts Lower House, of which he was a member, stated, "I thank God we have a Federal government. I have had the honor to move an address to the President. . . . It is not so sublime and sentimental as I could wish— but it is as good as ought to be expected from such a mixed medley as compose our General Court."[73] Sedgwick wrote soon after this, "Today I dined with the President and as usual the company was as grave as at a funeral. All the time at table the silence more nearly resembled the gravity of [illegible] worship than the cheerfulness of convivial meeting."[74] All the descriptions of Washington in office, but particularly those written during the first months of his Administration, when there seems to have been a conscious effort to set the tone for the new government, stress the formality of his bearing. A court etiquette was drawn up and strictly

[73] Henshaw to Sedgwick, Jun., 1789, Sedgwick Papers, MHS.
[74] Sedgwick to Ephraim Williams, Jun., 1789, *ibid.*

observed, and if the operations of the government had reflected the atmosphere which surrounded Washington, monarchy would have been only a little way ahead.

The genuine respect and gratitude which the people bore Washington and their realization of the momentous step being taken with the establishment of a new government offered an adequate basis for a certain degree of solemnity on state occasions. Apparently, however, this spontaneous regard of the masses of the people for Washington did not reach the heights of the "sublime and sentimental," and some who were most interested in the setting up of the new government deliberately strove to increase the influence of Washington in every way possible. He was to be lifted above the level of criticism, and the measures of the new government were to be linked inseparably to him. In 1793 Jefferson recalled an observation that Madison had made to him early in 1790, "that the satellites & sycophants which surrounded him had wound up the ceremonials of government to a pitch of stateliness which nothing but his personal character could have supported, & which no character after him could ever maintain."[75] Except that Hamilton, one of the chief movers in this political strategy, was no man's sycophant or satellite, Madison's judgment was accurate prophecy; and Hamilton himself would probably have admitted that to increase Washington's hold on the popular imagination was a necessary part of his plans. Certainly no one ever described the relation between them better than Hamilton did when after Washington's death he wrote, ". . . he was an *Aegis very essential to me.*"[76]

The isolation which was imposed upon Washington by the ceremonious manner in which he lived enhanced the importance of those believed to be in his confidence, while it rendered him more dependent than he otherwise would have been upon his advisers. Under the circumstances, the utterances of such men as Hamilton and Robert Morris, whose advice he was known to value, were doubtless believed by many to reflect the views of the President, while the opinions which such men gave Washington were probably regarded by him as those both of Congress and of the solid men of business. The stage setting for the new Administration, certainly so far as John Adams had a share in it, had probably not been designed with any such purpose as this in mind, but that this state of things was

[75] Jun. 9, 1793, Madison Papers, LC.
[76] Hamilton to Tobias Lear, New York, Jan. 2, 1800, Lodge, *Hamilton's Works*, X, 537, underlined in original.

among the more important effects of Washington's exalted position there seems no reason to doubt.

The very serious illness of Washington in his first year of office,[77] from which he had not been expected to recover, must have interfered seriously with his comprehension of the fundamental measures which were being discussed at that time. This illness, incidentally, made a deep impression upon those who were depending upon Washington's prestige for the establishment of a government to their tastes. Christopher Gore's estimate of his importance to the Union at this time is shown in one of his letters to King, written May 30, 1790:

These things [desire for discrimination between original holders and speculators], my dear friend, make me truly anxious that some men shou'd be bound to this government by strong pecuniary ties, and which ties are not obvious to the public view. Suppose a possible event, the dissolution of the President, wou'd not, unless some chain of more & stronger links than now binds the Union shou'd hold us together, the American people cease to exist as a nation—and let me ask what other chain so binding as that of involving the interests of the men of property in the prosperity of the government. . . .[78]

We have Madison's word for it that Washington himself believed the state of his health in these first years in office to be such that he should not be required to serve a second term:

He then entered on a more explicit disclosure of the state of his mind; observing that he could not believe or conceive himself any wise necessary to the successful administration of the government; that on the contrary he had from the beginning found himself deficient in many of the essential qualifications, owing to his inexperience in the forms of public business, his unfitness to judge of legal questions, and questions arising out of the Constitution; that others more conversant in such matters would be better able to execute the trust; that he found himself also in the decline of life, his health becoming sensibly more infirm, and perhaps his faculties also; that the fatigues and disagreeableness of his situation were in fact scarcely tolerable to him; that he only uttered his real sentiments when he declared that his inclination would

[77] J. C. Fitzpatrick, ed., *The Diaries of George Washington,* 4 vols. (Boston and New York, 1925), IV, 129, text and footnote. Washington's illness, an attack of pneumonia, kept him from making any entries from May 10 to Jun. 24, 1790.

[78] King, *Correspondence,* I, 388.

lead him rather to go to his farm, take his spade in his hand, and work for his bread, than remain in his present situation. . . .[79]

Washington made these remarks to Madison at a time when the worst trials of the Presidency still lay ahead of him. In 1792 party strife had hardly begun in earnest; the decisions which the conduct of England and France forced upon this country in 1793 marked the first serious and long continued dissension in the Cabinet. In his procedure with the Cabinet on difficult questions, Washington seems to have regarded himself only as chairman of a board.[80] At first he depended upon the advice of senators and members of the Supreme Court, but he later learned that they, and particularly the latter, did not regard it as a function of their offices to advise him upon questions of every kind. He then asked the written opinions of his department heads, and later began to have these department heads meet with him, but he took very little part in the discussions. He did not give his opinion unless the Cabinet of Hamilton, Knox, Randolph, and Jefferson was evenly divided. On the rare occasions when it was needed, his own opinion became the deciding one, but there is no indication that when these men were divided three to one, Washington ever followed the advice of the lone member, even though that advice happened to coincide with his own opinion. There was no parallel here with the procedure of Lincoln, who after getting the opinion of each member of his Cabinet, is said to have remarked, "Eight ayes, one nay; the nays have it."

As a general, Washington had shown more than customary dependence upon his staff. In a field in which he felt that he knew less than he did of warfare, he depended even more upon his advisers, and as the conflict between Jefferson and Hamilton grew more and more bitter and was taken up in pamphlets and newspapers, Washington probably suffered more than he ever had on any battlefield.

After Jefferson had withdrawn from the Cabinet, no one among Wash-

[79] May 5, 1792, Madison, *Letters,* I, 556-57. Madison called this "Substance of a Conversation with the President."

[80] For treatment of Washington's Cabinet see James Parton, "The Cabinet of President Washington," *Atlantic Monthly,* XXXI (Jan., 1873), 29-44; Thomas Jefferson to Walter Jones, Mar. 5, 1810, Paul Leicester Ford, ed., *The Writings of Thomas Jefferson,* 10 vols. (New York, 1892-99), IX, 273-74 (hereafter cited as Ford, *Jefferson's Writings*); Mary Louise Hinsdale, *A History of the President's Cabinet* (Ann Arbor, 1911), *passim;* Charles Marion Thomas, *American Neutrality in 1793. A Study in Cabinet Government* (New York, 1931), *passim.*

ington's intimate advisers represented a point of view sharply opposed to Hamilton's and there was little disagreement until in the summer of 1795 the question of ratifying the Jay Treaty arose.[81] Washington's relation to the struggle between the two slowly emerging parties changed after Jefferson's withdrawal, and this change coincided with or brought about an important change in the struggle itself. Until Jefferson had withdrawn, each party had been represented at court and could have a hearing.[82] The appeal of each side had to be to reason and, in order to move Washington, had to be put in terms which a mind in close sympathy with that of the average man of the time could grasp. When after Jefferson's retirement there was no longer any opportunity for the point of view of one side to be so expressed, there was no longer any necessity for the other side to strive to express itself in the same way. Each was then exposed to a temptation which it had not had to face before. Secret societies, subversion, and defiance seemed the only course possible to many who disapproved of government policies, since an opposition party had yet to be formed, much less to be vindicated in popular opinion. Reliance upon authority, the *fait accompli,* and, ultimately, force was the obvious answer to such procedure. From the point of view of the historian it does not matter whether force provoked subversion or subversion, force; the important thing for the development of parties is the way in which the attitudes of supporters and opponents of the Administration aggravated each other. It is obvious that if the course indicated by Shays' Rebellion, the Whiskey Rebellion, and Fries' Rebellion was to be followed, written constitutions would go for little and the actual mode of government would follow the old patterns of tyranny or disorder. At the time of these disorders substantial groups felt that they had no effective voice in the government, while many conservatives wished to see the disaffected areas treated like conquered provinces. This was one of the gravest problems of the period, yet Washington seems never to have thought of it in these terms. More than any other man of his time, he tried to prevent the growth of parties, holding that there was no necessity or place for them in our form of gov-

[81] See below, The Jay Treaty, part 2.

[82] The term "party" is used in this connection even though this study will attempt to prove that Jefferson was not at the head of a party from 1790 to 1793 in the sense in which he was from 1797 on. It is here used with somewhat the same connotation as "party to an argument." It will save many explanations if we call the groups holding conflicting points of view "parties" even before they are conscious of themselves as such.

ernment. Had he been successful in this, the main effort of his declining years, it is most doubtful that representative government in this country would have outlived him for long. He thought that republicanism was in grave danger from the tactics and behavior of the opposition party, but he apparently did not perceive any danger to these principles from Administration policies.

Small says of Washington's attitude in the last years of his Presidency:

In fact his observation as to the rapidity with which the populace was aligning itself with political factions and injecting itself into their violent yet petty disputes, tended to diminish his faith in the ability of people to discern its own good, and to confirm him in his opinion that he must henceforth endeavor to guide, rather than to reflect opinion.[83]

If Washington's conception of his duty changed, if he came to believe that he should "guide rather than reflect opinion," a very important question is raised. In what direction did he wish to guide it? His state of mind at this time may be seen in a letter concerning the Jay Treaty which he wrote to Knox in September, 1795:

Next to a conscientious discharge of my public duties, to carry along with me the approbation of my Constituents, would be the highest gratification my mind is susceptible of; but the latter being subordinate, I cannot make the former yield to it; unless some criterian more infallible than partial (if they are not party) meetings, can be discovered as the touch stone of public sentiment. If any power on earth could, or the great power above would, erect the standard of infallibility in political opinions, there is no being that inhabits this terrestrial globe that would resort to it with more eagerness than myself, so long as I remain a servant of the public. But as I have found no better guide hitherto than upright intentions, and close investigation, I shall adhere to these maxims while I keep the watch; leaving it to those who will come after me to explore new ways, if they like; or think them better.[84]

This letter shows that although Washington regarded the opposition to the Jay Treaty as the work of a "party," he did not regard the support of the Treaty as also being the work of a party. His desire to have a standard of political infallibility made known to him is also characteristic. Finally, while there can be no doubt of the purity of his intentions, there must be

[83] Small, *Some Presidential Interpretations of the Presidency*, 16-17.
[84] Mount Vernon, Sept. 20, 1795, Fitzpatrick, *Washington's Writings*, XXXIV, 310.

considerable doubt as to the nature and thoroughness of the close investigation of which he speaks. In the early years of his Presidency he received information about the state of public feeling from a wide variety of persons, but after 1794 he seems to have sought advice only from a closely restricted circle in sympathy with Administration policies.[85] This change was in a sense to be expected. As parties began to form and opinion became more and more divided, people naturally consorted more with their own kind than heretofore, but the more Washington followed this tendency, the more bitterly he denounced parties. He is to be blamed, not for allying himself with a party, but for not knowing that he had done so, and for denouncing those opposed to his party as opposed to the government. He was most in the grip of party feeling at the time when he was being represented as being above it.

It may be said that Washington was no more dependent upon Hamilton in the last years of his Presidency than he had been in the early ones, and that the two men were as thoroughly of one mind throughout this whole period as they are usually represented. It can be shown, however, that in the earlier years Washington had questioned Hamilton upon some of the most fundamental points of the latter's policy and that Hamilton had had to resort to evasion, if not outright deception, to answer. Washington wrote him a long letter in August, 1792, in which he sent him objections to the course the government was following, objections which had been put to him by George Mason of Virginia. Among the most searching of these was the following charge:

The funding of the debt has furnished effectual means of corrupting such a portion of the Legislature as turns the balance between the honest voters whichever way it is directed.[86]

Hamilton answered:

As far as I know there is not a member of the Legislature who can properly be called a stock-jobber or a paper-dealer. . . . As to improper speculations on measures depending before Congress, I believe never was any body of men freer from them.[87]

In the vote on Assumption, the most important measure of that time

[85] A comparison of Washington's letters from 1789 to 1794 with his letters from that time until his death is the basis for this statement.
[86] Quoted by Hamilton in his reply to Washington, Philadelphia, Aug. 18, 1792, Lodge, *Hamilton's Works*, II, 454.
[87] *Ibid.*, 456.

on which there is a record of the yeas and nays, we find material to challenge Hamilton's statements. Of the fourteen senators who favored Assumption, at least ten held securities. Of the thirty-two members of the House who favored it, at least twenty-one held securities.[88] Further, these security holders were the men nearest Hamilton. Can we believe that he did not know of the holdings of Strong, Ellsworth, Johnson, King, Schuyler (his own father-in-law), Read, Robert Morris, and Charles Carroll in the Senate, or of those of Ames, Sedgwick, Wadsworth, Laurance, Benson, Boudinot, Clymer, Fitzsimmons and William L. Smith, the members of the House who were most intimate with him? Some of these men were also very close to Craigie and Duer and were almost certainly among those whose chief interest in the financial measures before Congress lay in the promise of large profits for themselves. Can we believe that Hamilton did not know as much as Andrew Craigie of the speculations of congressmen in government securities, of their desire to postpone the funding of the debt until they were in the position to take full advantage of it? Whether these men could properly be called stockjobbers or paper dealers is beside the point, and that Hamilton did not consider their speculations on measures pending before Congress "improper" does not conceal the fact that he did not choose to state what he must have known of them to Washington, letting the latter decide whether it was proper or not.

In 1794 Hamilton was charged in the House of Representatives with having used money appropriated by that body for a purpose other than that which had been designated. There was no charge that the use of the money had been improper in any other respect, but the law declared that money must be used for the purpose for which it had been appropriated.[89] He claimed that he had had specific consent from Washington, both verbally and by letter, for the use to which he put the money. Washington answered the letter in which Hamilton sought to remind him of the spoken consent as follows:

I cannot charge my memory with all the particulars which have passed between us, relative to the disposition of the money borrowed. Your letters,

[88] Charles Austin Beard, "Some Economic Origins of Jeffersonian Democracy," *American Historical Review*, XIX, (Oct., 1913-Jul., 1914), 282-98, *passim*.

[89] The most penetrating and judicious account of Hamilton's conduct upon the occasion of the alleged misappropriation of funds is to be found in Albert Gallatin, "A Sketch of the Finances of the United States," which was written in 1796: "Upon the whole, the transaction was illegal, but no otherwise criminal than as it was illegal." Gallatin, *Writings*, III, 112.

however, and my answers, which you refer to in the foregoing statement . . . speak for themselves, and stand in need of no explanation.

As to verbal communications, I am satisfied, that many were made by you to me on this subject; and from my general recollection of the course of proceedings, I do not doubt, that it was substantially as you have stated it in the annexed paper, that I have approved of the measures, which you, from time to time, proposed to me for disposing of the Loans, upon the condition, that what was to be done by you, should be agreeable to the Laws.[90]

Hamilton stated that this letter was not satisfactory, and letters from Washington which gave more specific approval of Hamilton's operations with the funds in question were apparently produced.[91] The significance of this incident for our present purpose does not rest on Hamilton's use of the funds, but on the light it throws upon the relation between Hamilton and Washington. It is natural that Washington trusted Hamilton without knowing too much about the details of the transactions which he was called on to approve, but that he would afford Hamilton the means of clearing himself before an investigation while entertaining the misgivings as to the legality of his conduct which his letter to Hamilton suggests, is one of the points which cause us to ask whether we see Washington at his best during the years of his Presidency.

From this time on, Washington and Hamilton became more and more "of one mind," at least in appearance. We cannot know the means by which this unity was reached,[92] but the results of it were strikingly appar-

[90] Washington to Hamilton, Philadelphia, Apr. 8, 1794, Fitzpatrick, *Washington's Writings*, XXXIII, 318.

[91] For evidence of the extent of Hamilton's influence upon Washington at this time, see Edmund Randolph's account of the affair, Randolph to Madison, Lexington, Virginia, Jul. 9, 1811; and same to same, Charleston, Jefferson County, Virginia, Aug. 8, 1811, quoted in Moncure Daniel Conway, *Omitted Chapters of History Disclosed in the Life and Papers of Edmund Randolph* (New York and London, 1888), 217.

[92] After Hamilton's pamphlet against Adams appeared in Oct., 1800, the latter wrote the following to Dr. Ogden, Washington, Dec. 3, 1800: "This last pamphlet I regret more on account of its author than on my own, because I am confident it will do him more harm than me. I am not his enemy, and never was. I have not adored him, like his idolaters, and have had great cause to disapprove of some of his politics. He has talents, if he would correct himself, which might be useful. There is more burnish, however, on the outside, than sterling silver in the substance. He threatened his master, Washington, sometimes with pamphlets upon his character and conduct, and Washington, who had more regard to his reputation than I have, I say it with humility and mortification, might be restrained by his threats, but I dread neither his menaces of pamphlets nor the execution of them." Adams, *Works,*

ent. In the fall of 1794, Washington denounced the Democratic societies, charging them with responsibility for the Whiskey Rebellion though many of these societies had condemned it; and many gave yet another instance of their loyalty to the government by dissolving soon after Washington's attack upon them.

The Jay Treaty is the most striking example of a measure which could not have been passed without the fullest use of Washington's prestige, and it was, of all the measures of his Administration, the one he was most reluctant to accept. Although he deliberated long and anxiously before signing it, and although he wrote to Hamilton soon after he signed it that "it would seem next to impossible to keep peace between the United States and Great Britain,"[93] yet it was only by the use of his prestige that the people of the country could be brought to accept the Treaty. William Plumer has recorded that no arguments for the Treaty were so effective as the statement that Washington had accepted it, and that it must, therefore, be for the best interests of the country.[94] In March, 1796, the House of Representatives was deliberating upon the question of appropriating the necessary money to put the Jay Treaty into effect, and they voted sixty-two to thirty-seven to ask the President for the papers which would explain the negotiations for the Treaty. Washington refused their request sharply, and the address in which he did so was widely circulated and used to discredit the House of Representatives. Christopher Gore wrote of the reception which Boston gave the address, "The President's answer has been universally pleasing here, some have become so enamoured with

---

IX, 576. It is needless to say that there is no evidence extant which indicates that Hamilton controlled Washington by such threats as Adams describes, and it seems most improbable that he did. [*Editor's note:* If Adams was mistaken about Hamilton's use of "threats" against Washington's "character," he was nevertheless correct in sensing that the General's "regard to his reputation" gave Hamilton a lever which he employed with extreme psychological subtlety to get Washington to follow his advice (see Hamilton to Washington, Jul. 30, 1792, Lodge, *Hamilton's Works*, X, 7-8; cf. hint of the same technique, Nov. 19, 1796, *ibid.*, X, 209, and May 19, 1798, *ibid.*, X, 286). It seems likely that the appeal to Washington to resume the Presidency at the election of 1800 (it arrived as the General was dying, Dec., 1799) was cast in these terms.]

[93] "By these high handed measures of that government, and the outrageous, and insulting conduct of its officers, it would seem next to impossible to keep peace between the United States and G: Britain." Washington to Hamilton, Aug. 31, 1795, Fitzpatrick, *Washington's Writings*, XXXIV, 295.

[94] See Plumer's MS Autobiography, for comments in the fall of 1795 on the Jay Treaty, *passim*, Library of Congress.

the thing that they have had it printed in white satin and are having it framed and glazed."[95]

The main burden of Washington's Farewell Address, much of which was written by Hamilton,[96] is the condemnation of parties. Even the famous passages against foreign influence and alliances are important in that connection, as the French were at that time exerting themselves to get Jefferson elected in the hope that the Jay Treaty would not go into effect if he were made President. This warning, so frequently quoted to give the sanction of Washington to any kind or degree of isolationism, seems to have come mainly from Hamilton, whose measures and policies did more than those of any other man in the country to involve us in the current of European affairs.[97] There is no reason to believe that isolationism was the policy which Hamilton wished us to pursue, since the whole tenor of his policies was in the opposite direction. His words in this part of the address were political propaganda, an effort to appeal to two of the desires strongest throughout the country at that time, the desires for peace and for an independent foreign policy. Such an appeal also turned attention and resentment away from the situation in which the Jay Treaty had placed us. It was praiseworthy to warn against foreign influence in our politics; but, under the circumstances, to point the warning in only one direction and to warn against parties themselves on the eve of a Presidential election, in the terms which Hamilton put into Washington's mouth, was to become the tool of a party without apparently being aware of it.

Hamilton did not cease to use Washington when the latter had retired from office. As soon as he had news of the XYZ Affair, which brought us to the verge of war with France, he asked Washington to make a tour of the Southern states, where his presence might provide the occasion for demonstrations of loyalty.[98] Though Washington did not yield to Hamilton's request on this point, he did support Hamilton's claims to be second in command in the provisional army, against Adams's determination not to alter the precedence which Knox and C. C. Pinckney had had over

[95] Christopher Gore to Rufus King, Boston, Apr. 14, 1796, King, *Correspondence*, II, 58.

[96] To estimate the influence of Hamilton in giving the particular emphasis to the Farewell Address which it bears, compare the brief treatment of parties in Washington's Original Draft with Hamilton's Original Major Draft. Victor Hugo Paltsits, ed., *Washington's Farewell Address in Facsimile, with Transliterations of All the Drafts of Washington, Madison, and Hamilton* (New York, 1935), 168, 185-92, 194-98.

[97] *Ibid.*

[98] Hamilton to Washington, New York, May 19, 1798, Lodge, *Hamilton's Works*, X, 285.

Hamilton during the Revolution. Commenting on this matter later, Adams said that he was only Viceroy under Washington and that Washington was Viceroy under Hamilton.[99] This was the most notable instance during his Presidency in which Adams was thwarted by the prestige of Washington, but he put up with opposition from his Cabinet largely because he did not feel that he could challenge ministers who had been appointed by Washington. Had they chosen to resign over a question of policy,[100] as they threatened to do early in 1797, they could have placed Adams in an impossible position. It was not until he had been driven so far that he himself threatened to resign and turn the Presidency over to Jefferson, not until the questions at issue seemed to him to justify such a step, that Adams ventured to challenge his ministers.

The way in which Adams was weakened at this time by popular feeling for Washington may be indicated by the fact that in Pennsylvania some of the farmers who defied the tax collectors during Fries' Rebellion in 1799 believed that Washington himself was coming to lead them.[101] Actually, most of Adams's Administration was only a continuation of earlier policies, but because of the differences between the two men and because the country had been prosperous in the early 1790's and was not so in the later years of the decade, Adams was blamed personally by many for all the difficulties of the country during his Administration.

At the time of Washington's death, December, 1799, the High-Federalist leaders were trying desperately to find some way of dropping Adams from their ticket in the coming election.[102] Gouverneur Morris had decided that the only solution was that Washington should run again.[103] The letter in which he tried to persuade him to do so was either at Mt. Vernon or on its way there when Washington died. People were deeply stirred by his death, and the publications dealing with it in one way or another make up more than 400 titles of about 2,200 which came off the press in this country in 1800.[104]

[99] Quoted in Manning Julian Dauer, *The Adams Federalists* (Baltimore, 1954), 218.

[100] See Adams, *Works,* IX, 286, for his account of the threat of his Cabinet to resign after he was inaugurated if Madison were sent on the mission to France.

[101] See depositions of prisoners and witnesses in the Fries Trial, Rawle Papers, Pennsylvania Historical Society. The Papers are those of William Rawle, Federal Attorney.

[102] See Sedgwick to King, Nov.-Dec., 1799, Sedgwick Papers, MHS.

[103] G. Morris to Washington, Dec. 9, 1799, Sparks, *Life of G. Morris,* III, 123-25.

[104] This information came from Mr. Pietr Oliver of Cambridge, Massachusetts, who has made a bibliography for the year 1800.

Even after Washington's death, the High-Federalists continued to use popular feeling toward him as a weapon against Adams.[105] In the pamphlet which Hamilton wrote against Adams in the fall of 1800, his main argument for C. C. Pinckney was that he had many points of resemblance to Washington.[106] The Republicans were likely to regard Washington's prestige as their greatest stumbling block, but to the very considerable extent that the Washington legend was used to thwart and undermine John Adams, Washington was for practical purposes their ally. In the early days of the Revolution John Adams had put Washington and Jefferson on the road to fame, but his prestige and authority as President were gravely menaced by the figures he had helped to create.

The way in which Washington was regarded by some of his more eminent contemporaries only adds to the enigma of his character. One of the most measured and penetrating comments upon him was written by Jefferson in a private letter in 1814, which, since it is long and may be found in his collected works, will not be quoted here.[107] When we reflect upon the magnificent tribute which Jefferson pays Washington here and the regard which many other Republican leaders held for Washington in spite of the fact that they were opposed to him politically,[108] and then remember Hamilton's remark at the time of Washington's death, "He was an *Aegis very essential to me*," a statement which Benjamin Rush made about Washington's reputation takes on new interest. Rush wrote to Adams, "The detractors from the fame of most military men have been their enemies—the detractors from that of your character Washington are his personal friends, most of whom have lived in his family and re-

[105] High-Federalist strategy from Jan. to Oct., 1800, appears to have been to use Washington's prestige to support Adams and the Administration with the general public. Evidence to this effect may be found in Liston's letter quoted below, pp. 265-66, but Hamilton, at least, relied in part upon the appeal of Washington's name to bring Pinckney in ahead of Adams in the electoral vote.

[106] "The Public Conduct and Character of John Adams, Esq., President of the United States," Lodge, *Hamilton's Works*, VII, 309-64.

[107] Jefferson to Dr. Walter Jones, Jan. 2, 1814, Ford, *Jefferson's Writings*, 448-51.

[108] There was a middle ground occupied by many Republicans between the adulation which was professed for Washington and the abuse which Bache and some others heaped upon him. One instance of it may be found in the writings of William Maclay, who, while critical of Washington's views and usually opposed to them, wrote in his *Journal*, after having sat with Washington in his box at the theater, that he wished his dear children might have been there in his place. "Long might they live to boast of having been seated in the same box with the first Character in the World." Edgar Stanton Maclay, ed., *Journal of William Maclay* (New York, 1890), 31.

ceived favors from him."[109] Liston, the British Ambassador, who moved almost exclusively in Federalist circles, wrote only a little more than a month after Washington's death, "Notwithstanding this ostentatious display of regret and veneration, I find a great proportion of his apparent friends and intimate acquaintances more inclined to depreciate his merit than to exalt his fame, and he seems already to be in a great measure forgotten by the multitude."[110] It is doubtful if Liston had a sufficient knowledge of the facts to justify the latter part of his statement, but there could hardly be a better authority than he for the first part.

Timothy Pickering was one of the men who tried to exploit Washington's prestige but who did not regard him highly except in a moral sense. Years after Washington's death he wrote, "No man, however well-informed, was willing to hazard his own popularity by exhibiting the real intellectual character of the immensely popular Washington."[111] He thought that Washington's prudence and want of decision had been due to his realization of his own deficiencies and that while it was patriotic for those who were aware of his defects to have been silent on this point so as not to undermine public confidence, there was no reason why they should remain silent longer.[112] "But who originated the great measures of Washington's administration? Certainly not Washington."[113] Pickering gave Hamilton almost all of the credit and thought that if it had not been for Hamilton, Jefferson would have had an influence with Washington similar to that which Hamilton exerted.[114]

The description which Liston gave of the memorial ceremonies held throughout the country on February 22, 1800, illustrates some of the ways in which the official custodians of Washington's reputation used it after his death.

The day was solemnized by crowded meetings in places of worship,—processions of the legislature and other publick bodies, and the delivery of funeral orations, preceded by prayers adapted to the occasion.

---

[109] Rush to Adams, Philadelphia, Apr., 1812, Rush MSS, XXIX, 1, 20A, Library Company of Philadelphia, Ridgway Branch.

[110] Dispatch No. 3, Liston to Grenville, Philadelphia, Feb. 2, 1800. All letters from Liston to Grenville and Grenville to Liston used in this work are from transcripts of British State Papers in the Library of Congress.

[111] Pickering Papers, LI, 171, Massachusetts Historical Society.

[112] *Ibid.*, 226.

[113] *Ibid.*, 233.

[114] *Ibid.*, 234.

The leading men in the United States appear to be of the opinion that these ceremonies tend to elevate the spirit of the people, and contribute to the formation of a *national character,* which they consider as much wanting in this country. And assuredly, if self-opinion is (as perhaps it is) an essential ingredient in that *character* which promotes the prosperity and dignity of a nation, the Americans will be gainers by the periodical recital of the feats of their Revolutionary war, and the repetition of the praises of Washington. The hyperbolical amplifications, the Penegyricks in question have an evident effect especially among the younger part of the community, in fomenting the growth of that vanity, which to the feelings of a stranger had already arrived at a sufficient height.

The orators upon this occasion (who are generally attached to the ruling system of politics) have wisely seized the occasion to raise the publick esteem for the federal constitution, and to strengthen the hands of the administration of Mr. Adams, by dwelling upon the strong and unequivocal approbation which the late president gave to both. It is further to be remarked, to the honour of these gentlemen, that they have in general expressed themselves with less animosity and indecorum respecting Great Britain than used to prevail in discourses of an analogous nature on former occasions.[115]

The question of his relation to the development of political parties is not the vantage point from which a final estimate of Washington in the last decade of his life can be best given, however important the question is for the purposes of this study. In such a discussion we deal almost exclusively not with the elements of his greatness, but with the weaknesses which he probably would not have exhibited in his prime. Further, if we concentrate upon his political significance Washington himself is obscured and crowded out by the legendary figure which was so cleverly manipulated. An aged military hero who symbolizes national unity and independence becomes one of the most dangerous figures possible to representative government if he gets into the hands of a group who protect with the magic of his name whatever furthers their ends, and then use the denunciations of him which follow as a further political weapon. A political opposition must be very solidly based in order to survive the attacks which can be made upon it in this state of affairs. The extent to which this description fits the use made of Washington in his declining years is still to be decided, but the decision must be based upon a more

[115] Dispatch No. 10, Liston to Grenville, Philadelphia, Mar. 8, 1800.

scholarly approach and a much larger body of material than can be found in any of his biographies. The political exploitation of Washington's name in the first decade of the new national government has misled posterity even more completely than it did his contemporaries, and perhaps the most interesting question of these crowded years is how much Washington himself knew and what he really thought about the important policies and events of the 1790's.

II

Adams and Jefferson

1. JOHN ADAMS

JOHN ADAMS had no such simple and definite role in the growth of parties as had Washington, Hamilton, and Jefferson. Washington's greatest importance in this connection lay in the way in which his prestige was used to further Hamilton's ends, and Jefferson was important in the 1790's mainly as a center for the growing opposition to Federalist views and policies. Adams is not, however, the less important because his part cannot be described in such simple terms as these.

Adams was important both as a public figure and as a political theorist. In the former role his influence was largely negative, but in the latter he was perhaps the leading man of his generation. The two were not without influence upon each other, but the relation between them is perhaps clearer if we follow each separately.

Adams's part in the formation of parties was negative in the sense that he did not lead either of the two contending parties as did Hamilton and Jefferson, and he had no such popularity as Washington's to lend to the support of either party if he had wanted to do so. Yet it was Adams and the moderate Federalists who saved the country from war with France and probably from imperialistic adventures in the West Indies and Latin America in 1798 and 1799. If Hamilton had come to cherish the dream of a military dictatorship, as some have charged, it was Adams rather than Jefferson who at this, the most favorable moment, made it impossible.

The importance of Adams in the formation of parties lies in the fact that while by making peace with France he checked the plans of the most vigorous and reactionary of the Federalist leaders, he was unable to consolidate his own support and remain in power. His Administration gave the time and the most favorable circumstances possible for the crucial steps in the formation of the new party. Hence no story of the struggle between Jefferson and Hamilton can ignore him.

For the development of Jeffersonian democracy as a political movement, the four years of opposition from 1797 to 1801 were absolutely essential. Had Jefferson been elected in 1796, as he came so near being, he would have been regarded by many people not as President of the American people, but as the tool of France. This view would not have been just in 1796 or at any other time, but the Republicans badly needed the experience they gained as an opposition party in the years 1797 to 1801 for the development of both their principles and their organization. In 1796 their views were more doctrinaire and less indigenous to America than in 1800, and their organization too loose and insecure to have withstood the impact of the events of the late 1790's. By 1800 the country had had a better chance to learn its own mind. Many writers seem to believe that Jefferson was insincere when he voiced the hope that he would not be elected President in 1796, but those familiar with the circumstances ought at least to recognize the wisdom expressed in this hope.

The circumstances of Adams's Administration could hardly have been more admirably designed for the purpose of giving an opposition party under a popular leader a chance to extend its organization and disseminate its principles. Adams was succeeding Washington, and a period of economic depression was following one of general prosperity. His own personality, with his choleric temperament and his elaborate theories, each so difficult to understand and so easy to caricature, presented the opposition with an ideal target. In the South and the middle states, his opponents made the same sort of political capital out of Adams's "monarchism" as the New England Federalists made out of Jefferson's "atheism." Throughout the country his short, round person and his bumptiousness were contrasted in every mind with the stature and grave dignity of Washington.

It is customary when writing of the Presidency of John Adams to speak of him as a man of great gifts and great shortcomings, and then to concentrate upon the latter.[1] This approach has proved as satisfactory to those who favor Hamilton and the High-Federalists as to those who favor Jeffer-

---

[1] It is interesting to see the comment upon Adams as President by a man whose own difficulties of temperament are generally blamed for the failure of his greatest aspirations. Woodrow Wilson wrote of him, after mentioning Adams's services, ". . . but he was still the John Adams of the Revolution, stung by jealousies which he tried in vain to conquer, too sensitive, too hasty, too acid in judgment, erratic, intolerant, irascible, sometimes irresolute,—a man to trust in the long run and to stand loyal to with steady purpose, but not a man to love or to deem above parties." Woodrow Wilson, *A History of the American People,* 5 vols. (New York and London, 1917-18), III, 31.

son. During the 1790's both groups vigorously disparaged Adams, and it is easy to show many instances of error and ineptitude on his part during these years; but few historians seem to have asked themselves what course was open from 1797 to 1800 to a President who did not wish either to follow the High-Federalists or the extreme Republicans.

Adams's personal traits are only rarely the dynamic, activating forces of his Administration. They rather restricted, or conditioned, the way in which other men acted. For this reason, rather than because of any injustice done to him thereby, a detailed examination of Adams's shortcomings is misleading; for if we are too concerned with his irascibility, we tend to overlook the nature of the circumstances in which he found himself. If we grant that any Federalist who was President at that time would have had either to follow the program of the High-Federalists until it led to war with France, declared or not, or split the party to avoid such a war, we see how largely beside the point are those expositions of this period which rest mainly on charges of Adams's vanity and unreasonableness. It is not the conflicts of John Adams's personality, but the conflicts of outlook and purpose within his Administration which we should explore.

Whenever a well-established political party splits, the question of the relations between the leaders of the two wings becomes one of great interest. To what extent were their differences personal? To what extent was the break between them merely a final parting of discordant and ill-mated groups within the party? The Adams-Hamilton quarrel had been nourished for a long time both by personal differences and those of principle and policy, but here we shall take up the more personal and obvious aspects of the feud between them. According to Adams, Hamilton's efforts to undermine him began soon after the Revolution. "I once at midnight after 18 hours of fatigue in preparing dispatches after the Peace of 1783, inserted a vain journal intended for a private Friend, Jonathan Jackson, in my dispatches to Congress by which means Hamilton obtained fewel [sic] to feed the flame of his damnable malice."[2] If we are to believe Adams's account that Hamilton's hostility to him went back so far, perhaps it may be attributed to the fact that Adams was among those in Congress who, during the Revolution, supported Horatio Gates to replace Schuyler, Hamilton's father-in-law, in the campaign that ended at Saratoga.

At the first Presidential election, Hamilton went to a good deal of

[2] Adams to Adrian Van Der Kemp, Aug. 15, 1808, Pennsylvania Historical Society (hereafter, PHS).

trouble to reduce the number of electoral votes cast for Adams. He sent word to more than one group of electors that it was necessary that they drop some votes for Adams so that there would be no risk that he would defeat Washington.[3] Hamilton had no plan of defeating Adams as Vice-President and no fear that Adams would be elected President instead of Washington, but he wished to reduce his influence.

In 1792, on the other hand, Hamilton was afraid that Clinton might make a respectable showing in his effort to become Vice-President, so he aided Adams instead of hindering him; but his way of doing so was singularly arrogant. He thought Adams was remaining away from the seat of government too long, and wrote to him:

I learn with pain that you may not probably be here till late in the session. I fear that this will give some handle to your enemies to misrepresent. . . . Permit me to say it best suits the firmness and elevation of your character to meet all events, whether auspicious or otherwise, on the ground where station and duty call you.[4]

Many thought Adams personally opposed to some of Hamilton's most important measures, particularly to the establishment of the Bank, though he had done nothing to hinder their passing. Support of these measures was, in the early and middle 1790's, the cardinal point in Federalist policy; and as the election of 1796 approached, many in informed circles doubted that Adams would be called by his party to succeed Washington. Adams thought that Jay, Hamilton, Patrick Henry, or himself might be the candidate;[5] and as the Federalists strategically delayed until the last minute Washington's announcement that he would not serve again, an atmosphere of mystery surrounded the question. Presumably, as in 1800 when Hamilton's bitterness toward Adams had increased, Hamilton was induced to accept him as a candidate only because support for him was so strong throughout New England as well as in some other states, notably Maryland. Whatever his reasons, Hamilton accepted him as the nominal Fed-

[3] See Charles Francis Adams, ed., *The Life and Works of John Adams,* 10 vols. (Boston, 1850-56; hereafter, Adams, *Works*) I, 445-46, for an account by Charles Francis Adams of Hamilton's exertions to lessen the number of Adams's votes. See also *ibid.,* VI, 543, text and footnotes.

[4] Oct., 1792, Henry Cabot Lodge, ed., *The Works of Alexander Hamilton,* 12 vols. (New York, 1904), X, 28-9. Hereafter, Hamilton, *Works*.

[5] See Adams to his wife, Feb. 15, 1796, Charles Francis Adams, ed., *Letters of John Adams: Addressed to His Wife,* 2 vols. (Boston, 1841), II, 201-2; Feb. 20, *ibid.,* 203; Feb. 27, *ibid.,* 204-5; Mar. 1, *ibid.,* 206-7.

eralist candidate for President but began working quietly to get the electors to choose Thomas Pinckney, the nominal candidate for Vice-President, instead of Adams. *The Gazette of the United States,* the Administrative organ, ran a series of articles which criticized Adams harshly,[6] denying that he had any share in the great achievements of the preceding Administrations. Robert Troup of New York later described the conduct of Hamilton and its results:

There is no cordiality on the part of the President to Hamilton. During the last election for President, Hamilton publickly gave out his wishes that Pinckney should be elected President. These wishes were communicated both privately and publickly to the President, and have occasioned, I suspect, more than a coolness on the part of the President. I blamed Hamilton at the time for making the declarations he did, and I foresaw that evil would arise from them. . . .[7]

Jefferson disclaimed any intention of competing with Adams if the Presidential vote in 1796 were tied, and they resumed friendly relations briefly. This worried the High-Federalists very much, as they lived in constant dread of a coalition between them.[8] They recognized more clearly the similarity of views on some very important points held by Jefferson and Adams than have most later writers.[9] Within a month after Adams's inauguration, Elkanah Watson, a Massachusetts Federalist then in Albany, warned him that Hamilton, Schuyler, and their connection still cherished bitterness toward him.[10] Watson was particularly irritated because of the

[6] These articles appeared in the Oct. and Nov. issues of *The Gazette of the United States* (Philadelphia), 1796.

[7] Troup to King, New York, Nov. 16, 1798, Charles R. King, ed., *The Life and Correspondence of Rufus King,* 6 vols. (New York, 1894-1900), II, 466. Hereafter, King, *Correspondence.*

[8] See letters of Sedgwick to King, 1798-1800, in the Sedgwick Papers, Massachusetts Historical Society (hereafter, MHS), for one of the best accounts of Federalist apprehension of an agreement between Jefferson and Adams at the beginning of the latter's term of office (letters of Sedgwick to King for this period are copies, stitched together, only part of which have been published in King, *Correspondence.* Pickering clung to the idea that there had been a "corrupt bargain" between Adams and Jefferson in 1800 by which, if the mission were sent to France and he and McHenry were dismissed from the Cabinet, Adams was to get Republican support in 1800. Pickering, convinced of this himself, was still trying to get evidence for it years later. Pickering Papers, III, 332, MHS.

[9] Gilbert Chinard is an exception. Particularly in his *Honest John Adams* (Boston, 1933), he emphasizes similarities in the views of Jefferson and Adams.

[10] Watson to Adams, Albany, Apr. 1, 1797, Elkanah Watson, *Men and Times of*

ground upon which Hamilton put his preference for Pinckney. Judge Hobart, later a Federalist senator from New York, stated:

. . . that Hamilton had said, in his presence, that Mr. Pinckney would, under all circumstances, have been the most proper character for President, because he was a new man, and would not draw in his train the spirit of party. A curious assertion, truly, for the most decided party leader in America![11]

On the first important question which faced the Administration of Adams—that of deciding whether or not to send a new mission to France after the French had refused to accept General C. C. Pinckney as minister —Adams, Hamilton, and Jefferson each thought one should be sent, though each had arrived at this decision separately and had different reasons for urging it. Soon after this beginning to his Administration, Adams found that its future course had been charted for him by Hamilton. He has described the plan:

Mr. Tracy of Connecticut, who indeed was always in my confidence, came to me, I believe at the opening of the special session of Congress which I called soon after my inauguration, and produced a long elaborate letter from Mr. Hamilton, containing a whole system of instruction for the conduct of the President, the Senate and the House of Representatives. I read it very deliberately, and really thought the man was in a delirium. It appeared to me a very extraordinary instance of volunteer empiricism thus to prescribe for a President, Senate, and House of Representatives all desperately sick and in a state of deplorable debility without being called. And when I maturely considered the contents of the letter, my surprise was increased. . . . That letter, though it had no influence with me, had so much with both Houses of Congress, as to lay the foundation of the overthrow of the Federal party and of the revolution that followed four years afterwards.[12]

The first open clash between Hamilton and Adams, however, came over the question of the command of the provisional army which had been authorized because of the XYZ Affair. The fact that after Washington had

---

the Revolution; or, Memoirs, ed. by Winslow Cossoul Watson (New York, 1856), 346-47.

[11] *Ibid.*

[12] John Adams, "Letters to the Boston Patriot," Quincy, May 29, 1809, Adams, *Works,* IX, 289. The recommendations of this letter were: the sending of a new mission of three to France, Jefferson or Madison to be one; the raising of an army of 50,000 (10,000 cavalry); the Alien and Sedition Law; the spreading of taxes to as yet untaxed articles; and a national fast day.

been made Commander-in-Chief, Adams did not wish to give Hamilton superior rank over Knox and Pinckney, is generally known; but apparently
it is less known that there was a concerted movement to get Hamilton
made Commander-in-Chief instead of Washington. Abigail Adams, perhaps the only person who has left an account of this latter effort, wrote:

> I am glad you approve the appointment, as you must I trust, of Commander
> in Chief, tho' some were asserting every power and faculty for Col. H—n. The
> President decided without communication and sent in the nomination of the
> old General, without the least intimation what his own mind will be. He sends
> the Secretary of War on Monday with the Commission. You can hardly con-
> ceive what a powerful interest is made for H—n. I am surprized at the want of
> knowledge of Human nature. That man would in my mind become a second
> Buonaparty if he was possessed of equal power. Yet my opinion is singular,
> what is the sentiment your way? Would any man there like he should have
> been made Commander-in-Chief? . . . What I have written of Hamilton is
> between ourselves and in confidence. I should like to learn the opinions of
> others. What is Knox's, what is Lincoln's? Would they Have advocated his
> *being first?* I hope Washington will not decline—he must not, he cannot.[13]

Washington did not decline the first post; but he did support Hamilton's claim to be second under him, announcing that he would resign if he
were not given the position,[14] though when he first heard about the matter
he asserted emphatically that Pinckney should be offered the superior rank
rather than Hamilton.[15]

Apart from the question of the appointments of officers, the conflict

[13] Abigail Adams to William Smith, Philadelphia, Jul. 7, 1798, Smith-Carter
Collection, MHS. Several of the letters of Mrs. Adams in those MHS collections
which are open indicate that she made an effort to keep in touch with New England
sentiment on important points and that she occasionally tried to shape it.

[14] See Washington to Adams, Mt. Vernon, Sept. 25, 1798, J. C. Fitzpatrick, ed.,
*The Writings of George Washington from the Original Manuscript Sources, 1777-
1805,* 39 vols. (Washington, 1931-44; hereafter, Washington, *Writings*), XXXVI, 453-
62, for Washington's reasons for his insistence upon Hamilton. See also Washington to
McHenry, Mt. Vernon, Oct. 1, 1798, *ibid.,* 476-77; and Washington to Pickering,
Mt. Vernon, Oct. 1, 1798, *ibid.,* 475.

[15] Washington to Pickering, Mt. Vernon, Jul. 11, 1798, *ibid.,* 323-27. The struggle
between Adams and Hamilton over appointments did not end here. The Senate
defeated a measure to make Adams's son-in-law, William Smith, Brigadier-General,
giving the commission instead to William North of New York, one of Hamilton's
henchmen. This appointment seems to have surprised Washington, though it did
not outrage him so much as some that were made and some that were not made
by the Senate Military Committee, all of whom were close to Hamilton.

between Hamilton and Adams at this time might have been due to their different conceptions of the proper mode of defense for the country. Adams stated a few years later:

I have always cried, Ships! Ships! Hamilton's hobby horse was Troops! Troops! With all the vanity and timidity of Cicero, all the debauchery of Marc Anthony and all the ambition of Julius Caesar, his object was the command of fifty thousand men. My object was the defense of my country, and that alone, which I knew could be affected only by a navy.[16]

Whether the main emphasis should be put upon the army or the navy in preparing for war during the late 1790's was a matter of more than ordinary significance, and it raises several very interesting questions. Were Hamilton and Adams speaking for definite groups or interests in this country when each supported his favorite arm so strenuously? If the commercial and moneyed interests of the country, who are supposed to have supported Hamilton's views, were primarily concerned about a large army, and if the agricultural branch of the Federalist party, commonly regarded as Adams's chief support, were most interested in a strong navy, it would appear that each acted in a way contrary to what might have been expected. The merchants and the financial interests would be concerned in the insuring of vessels and would desire an uninterrupted flow of commerce. One might expect these men to want our commerce to have the protection of a strong navy. Farmers, on the other hand, might be expected to be more anxious that an army be raised for the protection of the country itself. It seems very probable then that Hamilton and Adams were not spokesmen of particular groups, but that they were expressing their own views. If Hamilton based his policy upon close collaboration with England, he may have thought that we could rely upon the protection of her naval forces. Adams, on the other hand, wished above all that we follow an independent course, as he feared and distrusted England even more than France.[17] To follow such an independent course we needed first of

[16] John Adams to Adrian Van Der Kemp, Quincy, Apr. 25, 1808, PHS.

[17] John Adams to James Lloyd, Quincy, Mar. 29, 1815: "For full forty years, three points have been settled in my mind after full deliberation.

"1. That neutrality in the wars of Europe is our truest policy; and to preserve this, alliances ought to be avoided as much and as long as possible. But if we should be driven to the necessity of an alliance,

"2. Then France is our natural ally; and,

"3. That Great Britain is the last power, to which we should, in any, the last extremity, resort for any alliance, political or military.

"These three propositions appear to me as clear, as obvious, and as demon-

all a navy; and events proved that Adams's judgment was superior to that of Hamilton, who wanted a large army, and that of Jefferson, who wanted neither.

Hamilton and Adams had differed on the best way to wage war. They differed even more intensely when Adams attempted to make peace. In February, 1799, Adams decided that the French government was showing "a disposition to do us justice," and he announced that he was accrediting William Vans Murray, then at the Hague, as a minister to treat with France whenever that government should give assurances that our minister would be properly received. Perhaps no President ever made an announcement which had such violent political repercussions. Hamilton's wing of the party, which included the most important members of Adams's Cabinet and the principal Federalist leaders in the Senate, had committed themselves entirely to a military program. They based all their calculations, both in foreign and domestic affairs, on the presumption that we should soon be fighting France. Adams's appointment of Murray, giving assurance that negotiations with France were possible and that war with her was not inevitable, took the ground from under the feet of this group and split the Federalist party. The appointment of Murray was an act of political suicide for Adams, but the logical culmination of his views as to our best policy and his conception of the duties of his office.

Whatever the state of feeling between the moderate and High-Federalists, the issue upon which they publicly broke was not a petty or personal one. The question whether or not we should join England in a war upon France at a time when France was willing to make amends for her previous conduct, called for one of the most important decisions of the early years of our government. An alliance with England and a war against France and Spain offered a most attractive opportunity for an imperialistic adventure. Increased trade with the West Indies and Latin America, perhaps a joint commercial monopoly with England of this trade, could be offered as an inducement to the seaboard, while expansion into Florida,

---

strable as any political principles whatever, and almost as any proposition in Euclid.

"Miranda's plot, Mr. Pitt's plot, and Mr. Hamilton's plot (if, indeed, he had any hand in it), was in direct opposition to my system, and wholly subversive of it. On the one hand, I was determined not to submit to the insolence and injuries of the French government; on the other, to enter into no alliance with Great Britain, nor any kind of connection that might embarrass us in making peace with France, whenever her government should come to her senses and show a disposition to do us justice." Adams, *Works*, X, 147.

Louisiana, and perhaps Mexico could be offered to the frontier. All these possibilities and perhaps others were in the mind of Fisher Ames, sage and spokesman for Massachusetts Federalists after he retired from Congress in 1797, when he said in July, 1798, "My faith is we were born for high destinies."[18] The adjoining Spanish possessions already exercised a very strong attraction, and if we were to follow the customary pattern of intrigue, war, and annexation, we should never have a better opportunity to do so. There was at that time no reason to suppose that we should be able to expand into them as peacefully as we finally did for almost fifty years.

Adams defended preparation for war and the actual hostilities with France, as far as both went, by claiming that the course he followed was the mean between the extremes urged by French and English sympathizers, and the only truly national course possible under the circumstances. By his determination to make peace with France at the first opportunity and to steer this country in the course of true neutrality for as long a time as possible, he has cleared himself of any suspicion of wishing to make the sort of opportunity for aggression abroad and for military control at home which the High-Federalists saw in a war with France. He showed, further, a conception of the national destiny which was as indigenous and American as that of the Republicans. It was Adams's tragedy that he did not know how to implement this view, to find a basis for it in popular support. Jefferson's conception of the true destiny of the country was the more well-rounded in that he had not only the theory of government, but the ability to grasp the implications of public opinion and to give it shape in policy which was necessary to support his conception. Adams's lack of these assets made his break with his party only the more spectacular. No issue between the Jeffersonians and the Federalists was more momentous than the subject of this quarrel between the two wings of the Federalist party.

The High-Federalist leaders tried by every means to make Adams give up the appointment of an envoy to France. He compromised to the extent of sending a mission of three men to be nominated in the place of Murray by the Senate, and the Federalist leaders then hampered and delayed the departure of this mission as long as possible.[19] It did not start until October, 1799, and Pickering's letters to Ellsworth, head of the mission, before

---

[18] Ames to Pickering, Dedham, Jul. 10, 1798, Seth Ames, ed., *The Works of Fisher Ames*, 2 vols. (Boston, 1854), I, 235.

[19] See Adams, *Works*, IX, 299.

the departure seem to have been calculated to dissuade him from going.[20]

Once the mission was on its way, the split in the Federalist party became irrevocable, and in November and December the High-Federalists tried to form a ticket which would exclude Adams.[21] They learned that he must be allowed to run again, as New England, and particularly Massachusetts,[22] would not submit to having him dropped. The bitterness between the two factions increased when, in the spring of 1800, Adams forced McHenry and Pickering to resign from the Cabinet. In the party caucus held in June, 1800, just as the Congressmen were starting home, it was agreed to support Adams and C. C. Pinckney equally; but in the following months the Hamilton faction devoted themselves to a strategic attempt to get Federalist electors chosen, and to get enough of these electors to drop Adams to make Pinckney President in his place.

In October of 1800 appeared Hamilton's famous pamphlet against Adams—the climax of the growing struggle between the two wings of the Federalist party, which had become so bitter toward each other that some members of each preferred the election of Jefferson to that of their foe within the party. Under these circumstances the publication of Hamilton's pamphlet leaves unanswered the question of whether or not Hamilton intended it to defeat Adams. Thus the quarrel between the two men was not only important in determining what the contending forces should be in the election of 1800; it may quite possibly have given a decisive turn to the struggle itself.

For several reasons no study of John Adams's political influence in the 1790's could be complete without some treatment of his political theories. As the Washington legend had a separate existence of its own, so Adams's theories had a career apart from, but not without effect upon, that of their author. There the resemblance ceases, for while the Washington legend made whatever Washington did or whatever could be connected with his

---

[20] Pickering to Ellsworth, Sept. 13, 1799, Pickering Papers, XII, 69, MHS; Oct. 4, 1799, *ibid.*, 152; Oct. 22, 1799, *ibid.*, 259.

[21] Samuel Eliot Morison, *The Life and Letters of Harrison Gray Otis, Federalist, 1765-1848,* 2 vols. (Boston and New York, 1913), I, 185.

[22] For Adams's strength in Massachusetts, see Higginson to Pickering, Boston, Jan. 12, 1800: "In the present State of things, no man would be appointed an Elector in this State, who would not throw away his Vote, or do anything else, which shall be thought necessary to secure Mr. Adams; and on that Subject be governed by the opinion of himself or his friends." Letters of Stephen Higginson, 1783-1804, American Historical Association (hereafter, AHA), *Report for 1896,* I, 834.

name seem wise and just, the popular conception of Adams's theories caused people to put the worst possible construction upon much that was done during his Administration. Another reason for concern with his theories is that they go far toward explaining his conduct, with its apparent shifts and inconsistencies; for Adams seems to have followed his theories instead of letting them be framed by his experience.

The first phase of Adams's thought,[23] lasting until 1783, was a highly practical one in which he gave much advice on the formulation of state governments, always warning against the unicameral principle. This was, nonetheless, the most radical period of his thought. It was characterized by his belief in the necessity of annual elections; and its larger purpose was to repel the encroachments of the King and Parliament, both of whom he believed to have ignored the true principle of the British Constitution.[24]

He showed at this time an attitude toward England which he was to retain the rest of his life. It was made up of two violently contrasting extremes. When he contemplated her institutions, "purged of their corruptions," as he usually stipulated, he was the political theorist standing in reverence before a unique creation. Neither Burke nor Blackstone had a deeper feeling for the slow evolution and organic growth of customs and precedents which had come to form a symmetrical whole. But when Britain was represented in Adams's mind, not by her ancient constitutions, but by the usual practices and policies of her eighteenth-century oligarchy, he was again a rebellious Boston colonial, not so different in attitude from his relative Samuel Adams. The attitude toward England of the men of this generation is very revealing. Hamilton thought that it was the "corruptions" of the British government which made it work; Adams, that purged of these corruptions the British government would be the best possible one; and Jefferson, that the true principles of the British Constitu-

[23] The comments on Adams's political theories have been based primarily on Adams's own comments upon them in his letters, though I have consulted Correa Moylan Walsh, *The Political Science of John Adams* (New York and London, 1915), and have carefully read Manning J. Dauer's thesis, "The Basis of the Support for John Adams in the Federalist Party" [*Editor's note:* published (Baltimore, 1953) as *The Adams Federalists.*] The latter presents Adams's ideas very concisely, and inasmuch as it is a study of more than his political ideas, it seems to be more solidly based than Walsh's work. The treatment given Adams's political theories in the present study is the conventional one; my main concern has been with the purpose that lay behind his political writings and the relation between these writings and his conduct.

[24] ". . . the King and Parliament committed high treason and rebellion against America," Adams, *Works*, X, 394.

tion had become so obscured and perverted that we were likely to be contaminated rather than guided by modeling ourselves upon it.[25]

All of his life Adams thought that the only good governments were mixed ones, that excellence in government resulted from a balance of the monarchical, the aristocratic, and the democratic principle. He always rallied to the defense of whichever of these principles he thought to be most in danger at the time. The second phase of his thought, which occupied him from 1783 to 1796, was marked by a defense of the aristocratic principle in government. In the last period, from 1796 on, he was the champion of the executive or monarchical element of the government against an aristocratic faction.

If we should confine ourselves strictly to the writings of his second period, Adams might seem the perfect spokesman for Federalism, particularly if we regard that movement as an effort to keep political control of the new government for the classes who had been dominant in the various colonies before the Revolution. It was his writings of this second period, from 1783 to 1796, which were so effectively used against him later. He never ceased to protest, however, against the construction put upon them; and in 1813 he wrote to Jefferson, "Now, I will forfeit my life, if you can find one sentiment in my Defence of the Constitution, or the Discourses on Davila, which, by a fair construction can favor the introduction of hereditary monarchy or aristocracy into America."[26]

That Adams wished to introduce monarchy into the United States was a common charge against him during the 1790's; and although the effects of this charge were not dependent upon its accuracy, it is interesting to inquire how much basis there was for it. Much of the feeling against his writings might be explained by his choice of terms. He often spoke of the monarchical and executive principles interchangeably, and because of this tendency he might easily pass for a confirmed monarchist among the literal-minded or those disposed to turn his words against him. On the other hand, as Manning J. Dauer points out, "To him democracy was always a system in which the people choose representatives to an all-powerful unicameral legislature. This he never ceased to condemn."[27] It should be noted that this is only a somewhat more emphatic statement of a view he

---

[25] Jefferson to Rush, Monticello, Jan. 16, 1811, Andrew A. Lipscomb and Albert E. Bergh, eds., *The Writings of Thomas Jefferson*, 20 vols. (Washington, 1903), XIII, 3-4. (Hereafter, Lipscomb and Bergh, *Jefferson's Writings.*)

[26] Adams to Jefferson, Quincy, Jul. 13, 1813, Adams, *Works*, X, 54.

[27] Dauer, *The Adams Federalists*, 50.

had held in his early, radical phase, from which he was supposed to have apostatized. Adams was sometimes more explicit and, when he was condemning this form, spoke of it as a "simple democracy."[28] Incidentally, a good many of the condemnations of democracy of this period arise from the fact that the men of the time used the term more precisely than we do now. They spoke of democracy as a form of government; we think of it as a spirit in which government should operate. Had they thought of it as an attitude of mind based upon self-discipline and characterized by respect for the rights and views of others, most of the conservatives of the Revolutionary generation would have felt differently toward it. They might have regarded talk of "democratic" government as visionary and utopian, but very few of them would have treated it with the contempt they so frequently show for the term as they understood it. The terminology which most conservatives of the period employed when they spoke of matters of government tends to conceal their thought from us, and that of Adams was particularly liable to misconstruction. Also, it may have been some of Adams's conversations or his speeches in the Senate upon which the charges that he was not friendly to republican government principally rested, for he was likely to say anything in the heat of the moment.

As far as Adams's political future was concerned, it was the sense in which his writings were understood that was important; but to approach the theories themselves properly, we have to understand Adams's purpose in expressing them. He believed that his mission was to reveal the true principles of government in an age of political experiment. Shays' Rebellion, the French Revolution, and other catastrophes foreseen by him could, he thought, have been or be averted if people would only apply certain principles of government which he believed almost as demonstrable as the propositions of Euclid. One of his accounts of the way in which he came to write the works of his second period may be found in a letter to Jefferson written in 1813:

. . . when Lafayette harangued you, and me, and John Quincy Adams, through a whole evening, in your hotel in the *Cul de Sac,* at Paris, and developed the plans now in operation to reform France, though I was silent as you was, I then thought I could say something new to him. In plain truth, I was astonished at the grossness of his ignorance of government and history, as I had been for years before, at that of Turgot, Rochefoucauld, Condorcet, and Franklin. This

[28] Adams to Jefferson, Quincy, Jul. 13, 1813, Adams, *Works,* X, 53-4.

gross ideology of them all first suggested to me the thought and inclination, which I afterwards executed in London, of writing something upon aristocracy. I was restrained for years by many painful considerations. . . . But, when the French assembly of notables met, and I saw that Turgot's "government in one centre, and that centre the nation," a sentence as mysterious or as contradictory as the Athanasian creed, was about to take place; and when I saw that Shays's rebellion was breaking out in Massachusetts; and when I saw that even my obscure name was often quoted in France as an advocate for simple democracy; when I saw that the sympathies in America had caught the French flame, I was determined to wash my own hands as clear as I could of all this foulness. I had then strong forebodings that I was sacrificing all the emoluments of this life; and so it has happened, but not in so great a degree as I apprehended.

In truth, my "Defence of the Constitutions" and "Discourses on Davila," were the cause of that immense unpopularity which fell like the tower of Siloam upon me. Your steady defence of democratical principles, and your invariable favorable opinion of the French revolution, laid the foundation of your unbounded popularity.[29]

Adams always viewed the outcome of the French Revolution, which issued first in a dictatorship and then in reaction—or the renewal of the Inquisition, as he called Metternich's system—as a justification for his warnings against it and as evidence of the soundness of his views. He prided himself on having opposed the French Revolution from the very beginning, and a fair specimen of Adams's view of his importance in the intellectual history of the late eighteenth century may be found in his own estimate of the influence of his writings:

When David Hartley returned from Paris to London in 1783, after the Signature of the definitive Treaty of peace with the United States, he went home full of ideas and hopes of a great revolution approaching in France in favor of Liberty and the Rights of Mankind; Hartley introduced me to Fox and Burke, who were his Patrons to whom he was an humble friend and a great admirer, especially Burke of whom he was the most perfect Idolater I ever knew. Burke, Fox and Hartley, with all others of their party were warm enthusiasts for the French Revolution, from 1783 to 1786. When the first volume of my Defence, was printed in 1786, I gave an elegant copy of it to Hartley and the other two

[29] Adams to Jefferson, Quincy, Jul. 13, 1813, Adams, *Works,* X, 53-4. See also Adams to Dr. Price, New York, May 20, 1789, *ibid.,* IX, 558-59, and Adams to Adrian Van Der Kemp, Jan. 30, 1800, PHS, for substantially the same account of his reasons for writing.

volumes as they came out. Hartley lent them to Burke; and they gave him his first suspicions and diffidence in the French Revolution. They produced an entire change in his views and sentiments; for the Organization of a free Government was a subject at that time as little studied by Burke, Fox, Hartley, Price and Jebb as by Turgot, Rochefoucault, Condorcet, and Franklin. After reading those volumes, a Gentleman in company with Burke, speaking of General Washington said he was "the greatest name in the world." Burke answered him "I thought so too, till I knew John Adams."[30]

Viewing the revolutionary movement in its world setting from 1789 on, we see that England, the country which took the lead in combating it, was also the one that produced both the classic attack upon it and the best known defense of it. Burke's *Reflections on the French Revolution*[31] and Thomas Paine's *Rights of Man*[32] came to symbolize the two sides of the struggle everywhere. Neither was the most defensible statement that could have been made of its author's position; but the declamation, the sweeping assumptions, and the disregard for logic which both exhibit reflected and stimulated the feeling of the period. Close reasoning would have had little appeal at that time. If Adams's writings really had the effect upon Burke which the preceding letter implies, they had a wider popular influence, even though indirect, than has been hitherto recognized.

It was upon the spread of the battle between Paine and Burke to this country that Adams's writings first became a matter for general controversy here. Burke was having a tremendous vogue, and Adams's *Discourses on Davila* had been running in installments in Fenno's *Gazette of the United States,* when in 1791 the first copy of Paine's *Rights of Man* appeared in Philadelphia.[33] The book had been sent over from England for John Beckley, who loaned it to Jefferson. Before the latter had finished it, Beckley requested that he give it to Smith, an editor who was to republish it. Jefferson, who did not know Smith, sent a note apologizing for its delay and ". . . added, *currente calamo,* that I was pleased to find it was to be reprinted here, that something was at length to be publicly said against the political heresies which had of late sprung up among us, not

[30] Adams to Van Der Kemp, Quincy, Jul. 5, 1814, PHS.

[31] Edmund Burke, *Reflections on the French Revolution and Other Essays* (London and New York, 1910).

[32] Thomas Paine, "The Rights of Man," Moncure Daniel Conway, ed., *The Writings of Thomas Paine,* 4 vols. (New York and London, 1894-1906), II.

[33] Claude G. Bowers, *Jefferson and Hamilton* (Boston and New York, 1930),

doubting but that our citizens would rally again round the standard of Common Sense."[34] The note, with Jefferson's name and official title of Secretary of State, was printed with the book.

With the publication of *The Rights of Man* in Philadelphia, under the apparent auspices of Jefferson, the battle of opinion opened in earnest in this country. John Quincy Adams, as *Publicola,* condemned Paine and Jefferson in the *Columbian Centinel* in Boston, and the authorship of these articles was generally ascribed to his father. Jefferson wrote to John Adams that he had had no idea that his note to Smith would be published, and disclaimed any intention of attacking him publicly.[35] Although Jefferson did not intend that his note be published and John Adams did not write the *Publicola* papers, these facts did not prevent the public from viewing the two men as the American equivalents of Paine and Burke.

Adams, while he sacrificed much popular favor, did not win the approval of the Federalist leaders by his part in this controversy. Hamilton was irritated that he had openly championed opinions which were so contrary to the general current of the time.[36] It probably seemed to him that Adams's contentions for the shadow of power would endanger his pursuit of its substance. Debate upon these abstract principles would only turn public opinion against Adams and those generally associated with him in the public mind. Hamilton, without revealing to the public his own views of what government should be, wished to settle each problem as it arose, in the way which would advance his construction of the Constitution and his scheme of government. He would get whatever popular support was necessary to do so by maintaining that his solution of the specific problem was essential for the maintenance of the government which had been set up and that the only alternative to his plan was the chaos of the Confederacy. He would thus be able to attack his opponents as enemies of the new government. In making his downright statements publicly, Adams exposed himself and his Administration as targets to be shot at. Hamilton, with no avowed purpose apparently except the support of the new government, had previously put his adversaries on the defen-

[34] Jefferson to Madison, Philadelphia, May 9, 1791, Paul Leicester Ford, ed., *The Works of Thomas Jefferson,* 12 vols. (New York, 1904), VI, 258. (Hereafter, Ford, *Jefferson's Works.*)

[35] Jefferson to Adams, Philadelphia, Jul. 17, 1791, *ibid.,* 282-85.

[36] Jefferson to Monroe, Philadelphia, Jul. 10, 1791. "Colo Hamilton, avowing that he never made a secret of his principles yet taxes the imprudence of Mr. Adams in having stirred the question and agrees that 'his business is done.'" *Ibid.,* 281

sive. Thus Adams's part in the controversy was dangerous to Hamilton's plans at this time when the Bank had not yet been established. The dangers to his economic program of the debate over Adams's political theories appeared in such items as the one signed *Republican* in the *Independent Chronicle* of Boston, which asked if speculators were to form our nobility. "If so 'Dukes, Lords and Earls will swarm like insects gendered by the sun,' and the worn-out soldier who had been tricked out of his paper would have the satisfaction of 'bowing most submissively to their lordships while seated in their carriages.' "[37] Adams's insistence upon general political principles which were obnoxious might very well lead to public discussion of the final effect upon our form of government of the economic policies being pursued. Had Adams's theories been widely disseminated before Hamilton's policies had been accepted and established, the latter would have been vulnerable to all attacks against the former.

As it was, once Hamilton's policies were established, Adams's well-known views served as the scapegoat, and the tide of popular resentment which later rose against his Administration resulted precisely from this situation. No one could have made popular the Alien and Sedition laws, the direct tax, and an army under Alexander Hamilton; but it is only when such policies as these could be represented as the logical outcome of the long-held views and sinister purposes of the chief executive that they put such effective weapons into the hands of the opposition as were presented to Jefferson and his followers for the campaign of 1800.

Until Adams broke with the High-Federalists, the latter were free to put through whatever legislation they chose in the knowledge that the popular resentment it aroused fell largely on a man that they would be glad to see disappear from public life. To the extent that the public contrasted Adams's Administration unfavorably with that of Washington, Hamilton's hand was, for the moment, strengthened. The Republicans, not daring in some cases to attack too openly measures which Washington was supposed to have favored, did their part in contrasting the two Administrations, and during much of his Presidency Adams was between two fires.

The whole story of the positions into which Adams was put as President by Hamilton's policies and of his conflicts with the Cabinet is only now becoming apparent, but it seems certain that it was these experiences which were responsible for the last phase of his political thought, in which

[37] As quoted in Bowers, *Jefferson and Hamilton*, 85.

he insisted upon the necessity for an independent executive who might check the aristocracy as represented by the Cabinet and the Senate. Adams had been in office only a few months when within the space of five days he wrote to two of his Cabinet members, Wolcott and Pickering,[38] warning them of the dangers of a divided executive. To the former, Secretary of the Treasury, he wrote in October, 1797:

> The organization of the stamp tax suggests a vexation to me. The bill was worth money, and money was so much wanted for the public service, that I would not put it at risk; otherwise I would have negatived that bill; not from personal feelings, for I care not a farthing for all the personal power in the world. but the office of the secretary of the treasury is, in that bill, premeditatedly set up as rival to that of the President. . . .[39]

Adams warned that this course would be followed "till we will have a quintuple or a centuple executive directory. . . ."[40]

If, as Sedgwick stated of Adams, his "pride is in never departing from principle,"[41] and if Adams from the beginning of his Presidency was forced to put up with what he regarded as the greatest abomination in government, a divided executive, why did he accept this situation until February, 1799? The answer is a complicated one. Adams was passing from one phase of his political thought to another, and that of the 1780's and early 1790's, marked by his defense of the *aristoi,* was perhaps the most congenial of all to him. For a time he was pulled in two directions; for the Republicans, French and American, irritated him much of the time even more than did the Hamilton wing of his own party. Practical considerations joined with these other factors to urge that he agree with the leaders of his party on all save the most important issues. Ultimately he did not shrink from the ordeal that awaits a President of the United States who does not have the support of his own party, but he did delay as long as possible that period in which his Administration would be disorganized and helpless.

Had he broken with the High-Federalists before the XYZ Affair put him in temporary agreement with the war party, and before the Alien

[38] Adams to Pickering, East Chester, Oct. 31, 1797, Adams, *Works,* VIII, 560.
[39] Adams to Wolcott, East Chester, Oct. 20, 1797, *ibid.,* 554-55.
[40] *Ibid.*
[41] Sedgwick to Henry Van Schaack, Philadelphia, Feb. 22, 1798, Sedgwick Papers, MHS. Sedgwick was explaining why Adams would not attend the birthday ball given in honor of Washington.

and Sedition laws and the Land Tax gave the Republicans issues with a wide national appeal, Adams and Jefferson would probably have joined forces against Hamilton. Those who regard this as impossible, who doubt that there could have been a union between the moderate Federalists and the Republicans, should remember the extent of this union after 1800, the support which both Adams and John Quincy Adams gave Jefferson after 1803-04, and the fact that the ever-present possibility of a coalition between the two was the High-Federalist nightmare from 1797 on.[42] Thus it would appear that one of the most important phases in the process of party alignment in the late 1790's was the struggle taking place in Adams's mind as to how far he would go with the High-Federalists. This struggle, even though we know too little about it, is as important a part of the story of party formation as anything in the plans or views of Jefferson and Hamilton. That Adams did not think of his decision in the light of its effect upon politics, that he was perhaps the one important man of his time who did "rise above party" on a crucial issue, does not lessen the importance of his conduct for the formation of parties.

We can best understand Adams's conduct at this time by considering his writings. That he wished to avert popular uprisings like the French Revolution and Shays' Rebellion does not mean that he possessed the kind of conservatism that was popularly attributed to him. If we study the purpose behind his writings, it is obvious that he would not go to all lengths with any group or interest. As we emphasize his purpose in writing, rather than his specific suggestions, his true position in the Revolutionary epoch becomes clear.

The picture of John Adams trying to avert Shays' Rebellion and the French Revolution by political writings, no matter what their merit, is one which seemed as ridiculous to those who wished to put down all such movements by any means as to those who wished to see them succeed and spread. However, when we remember Adams's ideal of balance and equilibrium as necessary to the well-ordered state, we see that he was addressing himself to those fundamental problems of society which still remain after an uprising has been crushed or a revolution successfully carried through. We may not agree with his means of realizing the end; but only

[42] Sedgwick to King, Stockbridge, Mar. 12, 1797, *ibid.* In this letter Sedgwick claims that Jefferson's letter to Madison, withdrawing his name from competition with Adams in case of a tie, was part of a plot to win Adams away from the Federalists.

those who, doubting that there are "natural" differences among men, believe in the practicability of the classless society, can logically deny the desirability of that balance, that precarious harmony between opposing groups and conflicting interests which Adams so earnestly sought. If we consider either his physical appearance or many aspects of his temperament, John Adams might seem as unlikely a vessel for the spirit of balance, order, and moderation as could be found, but these things he represented in the intellectual sphere as surely as Washington at his best did in more obvious ways. Usually frustrated and frequently ludicrous in the political world of management and intrigue, there is no reason to deny Adams the place he felt to be his on the intellectual and moral plane.

2. THOMAS JEFFERSON

Adams was hampered throughout his term by opposition both within and outside his party; and Hamilton, although he bent the twig and inclined the tree as no other single person has done, regarded his work as a mere beginning. A popular movement for which each had some measure of contempt interrupted the public services of both. This popular movement brought its own handicaps and limitations; it did not leave the man it brought to power so free to act as is generally assumed. Yet the fact remains that Jefferson did have opportunities for political self-realization greater than those of most Presidents, and that his fundamental aims and purposes have given rise to more controversies than those of any other of our great figures.

To many, there seems to be a fundamental contradiction between the aims which Jefferson and his party professed while in opposition and those which they pursued during his Presidency. This alleged contradiction serves as the basis for the charges by his detractors that Jefferson was an ambitious, unscrupulous demagogue; and even such an admirer as Herbert Agar states that "Jefferson by his failure to define his own intentions, prevented himself from winning a trial for his system."[43] Many who are on the whole favorably disposed toward him seem to have concluded that he was temperamentally unfitted for the executive position, and so made little attempt to defend his conduct while in office.[44] In this connection it is instructive to remember Jefferson's statement, made while Washington was President, that no man would ever carry from that office

[43] Herbert Agar, *The People's Choice* (Boston and New York, 1932), 55.
[44] Dumas Malone on Jefferson, Allen Johnson and Dumas Malone, eds., *Dictionary of American Biography* (New York, 1928-36). Hereafter, DAB.

the reputation he brought to it. This proved to be an accurate prophecy for Washington, Adams, Jefferson himself, and Madison. Yet, whatever the difficulties of the office, whatever may have been Jefferson's success or failure in it, the question remains whether or not he sought the same ends while in office that he appeared to seek in opposition.

Years after his retirement he continued to speak of "the Revolution of 1800," and the words would imply that he himself thought his election and Administration of some fundamental importance. Anyone, therefore, who deals with Jefferson's career as a whole must decide whether he failed to define his intentions or we have failed to understand them. Did he so far fail to meet the situation with which he was confronted as not to give his system a fair trial, or did he merely fail to solve for us, before they arose, the problems with which a representative government is constantly faced? We should keep these questions in mind while following the development of his political purposes during the years when the movement he was to lead was taking shape.

In the early 1790's Hamilton led a group of powerful men who knew precisely what they wanted and felt sure they could obtain it under the new government. The policies which they pursued seemed to Madison, Jefferson, and many others to introduce into this country the worst evils from which England suffered in a period when its government was in one of its most reactionary phases and its society highly stratified, and to threaten the republican principles which Jefferson and his colleagues believed should guide our development. Thus in the first phases of the party conflict we see a group which knew what it wanted and one which knew only what it did not want. What Jefferson did not want was a European society with its castes and artificial distinctions, its wars and hardships which made every man "either hammer or anvil." The only alternative to this, on a new continent peopled by European immigrants, was a type of society which had not existed before. Insofar as his goal was new, it was of necessity vague when compared with the concreteness of Hamilton's. Definition means limitation, and Jefferson's limitless hopes for the future of mankind are no irrefutable evidence of either the philosophical anarchy or the intellectual confusion with which he is sometimes charged. He saw a new continent of boundless resources and possibilities; he saw science opening new vistas in every direction; and he felt himself one with a new, free race of men who produced what they consumed and to whom servility and oppression were strangers. This new world, he thought, did not need to repeat the errors of the old, but he feared that it would if we were connected too closely with any European country or if we imitated their principles of government. He would probably have said that neither he nor anyone else should try to shape the future of the country. If he could do something to level the immediate barriers, to keep open and widen the path, he would have realized his purposes. Jefferson's chief intention for this country in the 1790's was the natural, unhampered development of a free people under a genuinely representative government, and he did not fail to define his intention repeatedly. His view was like that of Franklin, who, when asked what the newly invented balloon was good for, asked in return what a newborn baby was good for.[45]

Jefferson shared the basic assumption of the Enlightenment, that the great advances which science had made in the preceding century and a half were only the beginnings, and that they would better man's condition in other realms as well as in the physical. Whatever benefits science had in store which might affect society and improve human relations would, he thought, be long obstructed by the weight of tradition and inertia in Europe; but he was hopeful that here, where nothing had set and hardened, we might yet mold our institutions by reason. Conservative in some respects, Jefferson was a true revolutionary in his belief that human nature is molded by its circumstances and will reflect improvements in its conditions. Human nature is thus, man has always behaved so: these were not for him magic formulae, and the past not a prison from which escape was impossible. Our national independence, our isolation from Europe, which he would have fostered in every respect except the exchange of ideas and opinions, and the conditions and capacities of our people, which he thought favorable to the creation of a new type of society—these were to Jefferson the auspicious circumstances in which the new spirit was to work. Government might maintain or further these conditions by an abnegation of all save its minimum functions. It could do no more. The only real advances could come from science, education, philosophy, the means by which man enriches and improves himself. The temper of Jefferson's political thought is being constantly misrepresented by those who emphasize the negative role which he assigned to government, without further pointing out the forces upon which he would have depended for order and discipline in society.

Jefferson's interest in science was misunderstood by many in his own

---

[45] Carl Van Doren, *Benjamin Franklin* (New York, 1938), 700.

time, and its full implications still elude us. While specific achievements of his in mathematics, architecture, and invention are evidence of an amazing versatility, they are even more startling as evidence of unity and direction of purpose. His lifelong concern with science was not primarily due to breadth of interest; it was rather the measure of his centrality and integration. Jefferson was not the jack-of-all-trades or the incessant dabbler he is so often pictured as being; he was, rather, an exponent of the application of reason and common sense to problems of every sort. He thought of science as a new liberating force which had come into the world; and it was upon the revelations of science, with its attacks upon supernatural sanctions and hoary superstitions, that he based his view of government and society. His two basic concerns, the advancement of learning and the practice of good government, were devoted to the same end, to benefit mankind. They do not show any dual purpose; the latter was simply an effort to apply, in the most difficult and important field of all, the conclusions which he drew from the former.

Two letters, one written from France in 1789, the other ten days before he died, show the way in which interests usually regarded as diverse were linked together in Jefferson's mind. In the letter to President Willard of Harvard, accepting the degree of Doctor of Laws which that university had conferred upon him, Jefferson indicated the great opportunities for science in the United States, and concluded his letter:

It is for such institutions as that over which you preside so worthily, sir, to do justice to our country, its productions and its genius. It is the work to which the young men, whom you are forming, should lay their hands. We have spent the prime of our lives in procuring them the precious blessing of liberty. Let them spend theirs in showing that it is the great parent of science and of virtue; and that a nation will be great in both, always in proportion as it is free.[46]

Thirty-seven years later, in the last letter of his life, he wrote:

All eyes are opened, or opening, to the rights of man. The general spread of the light of science has already laid open to every view the palpable truth, that the mass of mankind has not been born with saddles on their backs, nor a favored few booted and spurred, ready to ride them legitimately, by the grace of God.[47]

[46] Jefferson to President Willard of Harvard, Mar. 24, 1789, Henry Stephens Randall, *The Life of Thomas Jefferson*, 3 vols. (New York, 1858), I, 537-38.

[47] Jefferson to Roger C. Weightman, Jun. 24, 1826, Lipscomb and Bergh, *Jefferson's Writings*, XVI, 182.

From these, as well as from many other quotations, we see that Jefferson thought of freedom as the necessary condition for intellectual and moral growth and of liberty as the true soil of science, which in turn revealed and strengthened the foundations of representative government. If it be said that science does not necessarily do so and that Jefferson's principles of government have no more validity than the optimistic eighteenth-century assumptions on which they rest, we may answer that the attacks on reason and objectivity sometimes made in the name of science, to which our own generation has been exposed, do not necessarily provide us with the last word on the problem.

Jefferson's belief in science and in reason was not the mere ornament of his learning. It was the basis of his life and conduct. Nowhere can we so clearly see the relation of his convictions on these subjects to the rest of his thought as in his view of the issues at stake when the party conflict reached its crisis in the late 1790's and the introduction of a military regime threatened to follow the Alien and Sedition laws. These circumstances confirmed Jefferson in his belief that representative government could not be crushed without a general attack on all fronts against the principles upon which he had depended to form the future of the country. He concluded a letter to one college student who had asked his advice on a course of scientific study:

I join you therefore in regarding as cowardly the idea that the human mind is incapable of further advances. This is precisely the idea which the present despots of the earth are [illegible] and their friends here reechoing & applying especially to religion and politics, that it is not probable that anything better will be discovered than what was known to our fathers. We are to look backwards then and not forwards for the improvement of science & to find it amidst feudal barbarism and the fires of Spitalfields. but thank heaven the American mind is already too much opened to listen to these impostures, and while the art of printing is left to us, science can never be retrograde; what is once acquired of real knowledge can never be lost. to preserve the freedom of the human mind then & freedom of the press, every spirit should be ready to devote itself to martyrdom; for as long as we may think as we will & speak as we think, the condition of mankind will proceed in improvement. the generation which is going off the stage hath deserved well of mankind for the struggles it has made & for having arrested that course of despotism which had overwhelmed the world for thousands & thousands of years. if there seems to be danger that the ground they have gained will be lost again, that danger comes from the generation of your contemporaries, but that the enthusiasm which characterizes youth should lift its parricide hands against freedom & science would be such a monstrous phenomenon as I cannot find among possible things in this age and country. Your college [William and Mary] at least has shown itself incapable of it, and if the youth of any other place have seemed to rally under other banners it has been from delusions which they will soon dissipate.[48]

To Elbridge Gerry he wrote in January, 1799:

I am for freedom of religion, & against all maneuvres to bring about a legal ascendancy of one sect over another: for freedom of the press, & against all violations of the constitution to silence by force & not by reason the complaints or criticisms, just or unjust, of our citizens against the conduct of their agents. And I am for encouraging the progress of science in all it's branches; and not for raising a hue and cry against the sacred name of philosophy; for awing the human mind by stories of raw-head & bloody bones to a distrust of its own vision, & to repose implicitly on that of others; to go backwards instead of forwards to look for improvement; to believe that government, religion, morality, & every other science were in the highest perfection in ages of the darkest ignorance, and that nothing can ever be devised more perfect than what was established by our forefathers.[49]

To Priestley he wrote a year later:

The Gothic idea that we are to look backwards instead of forwards for the improvement of the human mind, . . . is worthy of those bigots in religion & government, by whom it has been recommended, & whose purposes it would answer.[50]

Such passages as these demand repetition, because so little weight has been put upon them in connection with the study of Jefferson's party leadership. His basic convictions were at stake in his struggle against the Federalists. His ideas on states' rights and consolidation, on the proper relation between the executive and the legislative powers, by which the last generation of historians explained his part in this struggle, or the

[48] Jefferson to William Green Mumford, 1799, Jefferson Papers, v. 105, Library of Congress (hereafter, LC).
[49] Jefferson to Elbridge Gerry, Philadelphia, Jan. 26, 1799, Ford, *Jefferson's Works,* IX, 18-19.
[50] Jefferson to Joseph Priestley, Jan. 27, 1800, *ibid.,* 104.

economic motivations of his conduct which form more recent explanations, do not go very deep. Jefferson is at his most profound and most consistent in his views on what he called in his First Inaugural Address "the contest of opinion." This phrase introduces us to the most neglected aspect of our history of the 1790's, and points out a division of American society which reflected the intellectual and social movements then convulsing Europe. But Jefferson's fundamental concern with the future of republicanism did not, during the first years of this decade, automatically make him the party leader he is commonly assumed to be.

Jefferson was a late recruit to an opposition already led by James Madison, who first seriously opposed Hamilton's program in January and February, 1790, before Jefferson reached New York after his long absence in France. During the early 1790's, and until the election of 1796, it was Madison who was regarded by many Federalists as their principal adversary; and it was Madison who was far more determined in his opposition to Hamilton and his program than Jefferson. On such issues as Assumption—passed, it should be remembered, only with Jefferson's support—the question of our Neutrality Proclamation of 1793, and Jefferson's suggested overtures to Adams, early in 1797 (which would have tended to obliterate the distinctions between Republicans and moderate Federalists), we find Madison's position one of sharper antagonism to the Federalists than that of Jefferson. Indeed, the Secretary of State's first clear-cut opposition to a Hamiltonian measure came in the form of an opinion, which Washington had requested, on the constitutionality of the bill to establish the Bank of the United States. Jefferson had had no part at all in stirring up the widespread public sentiment against Funding, Assumption, the Excise—measures already agitating opinion before the Bank was even mentioned. If we recall the alarm at Hamilton's measures felt by some of those nearest him, we need not suppose any organized group to have been behind much of the public opposition to them.

A great deal of the work usually attributed to Jefferson in organizing opposition to Federalist measures, both in the House of Representatives and among the general public, should be credited instead to John Beckley, first Clerk of the House of Representatives, 1789 to 1797, and first Librarian of Congress, 1802 to 1807. Beckley, a native of Virginia, had been sent to Eton, where he is supposed to have been a friend of the younger Fox. He returned to this country and attended William and Mary.[51] In 1779

[51] The best source for the facts of Beckley's life is Hugh Blair Grigsby, *The*

he became a member of the first chapter of Phi Beta Kappa to be established, and he took part in its debates upon such questions as "whether a wise state hath any interest nearer at Heart than the Education of the Youth," or "whether Commonwealths or Monarchies are most subject to Seditions and Commotions."[52] He was enrolled in the Williamsburg Lodge of Masons,[53] which had a very close connection with the College at this time[54] and numbered among its members some who were to become prominent Republicans later.[55] He was Clerk of the Virginia House of Delegates from 1779 to 1789, and it was apparently with the help of Madison that he became Clerk of the House of Representatives on April 1, 1789.[56]

Early in the second session of the first Congress, Senator Maclay of Pennsylvania noted of the Virginia men, "Buckley [sic] and Madison govern them."[57] Maclay's earlier note on the intimacy of Beckley with Muhlenberg of Pennsylvania,[58] the Speaker of the House, would indicate that Beckley was aware of the decisive position which the Pennsylvania delegation would have in the vote on Hamilton's measures and was trying to combine them with the Virginian as a solid nucleus of opposition. He showed throughout the 1790's great awareness of the strategic position of Pennsylvania and later devoted himself to winning that state for the new party. Madison fulfilled one function of an opposition leader in that his attacks on Administration measures were so solidly based that they served to rally support, but he did not undertake to marshall opposition forces in the way in which Sedgwick led those who supported Hamilton's measures. Beckley gradually took over work of this sort and became something of a party whip before the party division had proceeded very far. He endeavored to get members back to the sessions promptly, and by the time

---

History of the Virginia Federal Convention of 1788, 2 vols. (*The Collections of the Virginia Historical Society* [New Series], IX, X, Richmond, 1890), I, 63, note 74. Hereafter, Grigsby, HVFC.

[52] "Original Records of the Phi Beta Kappa Society," *William and Mary Quarterly*, 1st ser. (April, 1896), IV, 215 ff.

[53] Grigsby, HVFC, I, 18.

[54] *Ibid.*, I, 17.

[55] *Ibid.*

[56] See letter of Beckley to Madison, New York, Mar. 13, 1798, Madison Papers, LC.

[57] Edgar Stanton Maclay, ed., *Journal of William Maclay* (New York, 1890), Jan. 31, 1790.

[58] *Ibid.*, Jan. 17, 1790.

of the Jay Treaty he was writing letters in an attempt to put pressure through their constituents on representatives he thought shaky. He was one of those most active in organizing throughout the country the public meetings which protested against the Jay Treaty, and he appeared in the election of 1796 to have been the most energetic organizer of public opinion in support of Jefferson. It was Beckley's clerk, Lambert, who accompanied Monroe, Muhlenberg, and Venable to the conference at which Hamilton told of his connection with Mrs. Reynolds, and both Monroe[59] and Sedgwick[60] stated that it was Beckley who was responsible for making this affair public, as Sedgwick claimed, through a desire for revenge for having lost his position in the House. He appears to have been ousted from his clerkship because of his activity in the election of 1796.

In addition to organizing the opposition, Beckley may have had some importance in preparing Jefferson for the role he was to play. During the years 1792-93 Beckley was giving Jefferson information about "paper men" and other speculators, and telling him of Hamilton's special favors to them and of the latter's intimate connection with the British.[61] In view of the general belief that it was Jefferson who first began to disseminate such stories and that he engaged Freneau to spread them broadcast, it is interesting to note that Jefferson appears to have been skeptical of what he heard. Of one such piece of information he wrote later, "[Hamilton] was far above that,"[62] and he noted that Beckley was reliable concerning what he stated of his own knowledge, but that he was too credulous and suspicious.[63] How much Jefferson was influenced by news which Beckley brought him, it is impossible to state; but it is significant that during the years 1792-93, as far as we can learn from trustworthy material, there appears to have been considerable influence exerted upon Jefferson in the attempt to bring him into opposition to Hamilton.

If we are to form a theory of the organization of the Republican party upon the reliable evidence which remains, we shall have to abandon the view that opposition to Hamilton's measures in the early 1790's was in

[59] Monroe to Burr, Albemarle, Virginia, Dec. 1, 1797: "You know I presume that Beckley published the papers in question. By his clerk they were copied for us. It was his clerk who carried a copy to H. who asked as Venable says whether others were privy to the affair. B. told H. that he considered him self under no injunction not to publish the business." PHS.

[60] Sedgwick to King, Philadelphia, Jun. 24, 1797, Sedgwick Papers, MHS.

[61] "Anas," Ford, *Jefferson's Works*, I, 265, 267, 274-77, 278-79.

[62] *Ibid.*, 275 *n*.

[63] *Ibid.*, 277.

any large degree dependent upon Jefferson. Statements such as that of Herbert Agar, that in "this year [1792] Jefferson and Madison set to work to organize the small farmers of the South and Western borders everywhere,"[64] or such accounts of the organization of the party as are given by Bowers in his chapter "Jefferson Organizes,"[65] must be regarded, in the light of extant authentic materials, as resting almost wholly on conjecture.

Bowers lumps together all those who, in their respective states, opposed the Federalists and implies, where he does not state, that their opposition was in some way due to co-operation with Jefferson. He completely disregards chronology and treats men who became active Republicans only in 1798-99 or 1800 as though they had become part of a closely integrated group which had centered around Jefferson from the early 1790's on. The men Bowers mentions by name in this connection are Samuel Adams, John Rutledge, John Taylor, Willie Jones, Charles Jervis, Ben Austin, James Sullivan, Abraham Bishop, John Pintard, Gideon Granger, Ephraim Kirby, John Langdon, Matthew Lyon, Aaron Burr, Nathaniel Macon, Timothy Bloodworthy, James Jackson, John Francis Mercer, and the Clintons and Livingstons. There are comparatively few of these men with whom Jefferson corresponded before 1797-98, and to many of them he never wrote.

Actually, during Washington's first Administration neither Jefferson nor anyone else in the United States conceived of the sort of popular party which he was later to lead.[66] By 1791 or early 1792, Jefferson began to oppose Hamilton's measures, but it was not until some years after that he assumed leadership of the opposition party. It is not until the summer of 1795, when numerous and highly successful mass meetings were being held from Georgia to New Hampshire to protest against the Jay Treaty, that we can see even the outlines of a popular party on a national basis. No evidence has yet been produced which would connect Jefferson in any way with the organization of these meetings. They represent the first general, organized protest against an Administration measure, and they

[64] Herbert Agar, *The Pursuit of Happiness: The Story of American Democracy* (Boston, 1938), 39.

[65] Bowers, *Jefferson and Hamilton*, 140-61.

[66] "Jefferson looked with favor upon the growth of the Republican party through democratic organization, but he was at a loss to suggest any methods of procedure, since he came from the South, where the township county system which was essential to the county convention, did not exist." George Daniel Luetscher, *Early Political Machinery in the United States* (Philadelphia, 1903), 3.

alarmed Federalist leaders as did few other events of the decade. The Democratic societies appear to have been the only existing opposition organized on a national basis while Jefferson was in the Cabinet, and no connection has ever been traced between them and Jefferson or Madison. In addition to this fact, it must be remembered that Jefferson was not so apprehensive then as he later became over Hamilton's plans and measures. He thought that Hamilton and his followers could not get the support of very many people and that if he ventured upon anything very dangerous to republican government he would, by losing the esteem of Washington, overreach and destroy himself politically. It was apparently the handling of the Whiskey Rebellion, Washington's denunciation of the Democratic societies, the terms of the Jay Treaty, and the means by which it was passed, which led Jefferson to believe that Hamilton would not keep within the bounds laid down by public opinion and that Washington was under his influence as he had not been in earlier years.

Jefferson's part in the setting up of Freneau's newspaper, in which, again, Madison took the lead, is frequently given as evidence of his early participation in party organization. Had Madison been under Jefferson's thumb as he is commonly represented, the question of who engaged Freneau would not be important. As it is, the fact that Madison took the lead in inducing Freneau to establish a newspaper at Philadelphia would indicate both his greater intimacy with Freneau and his more active opposition to the Administration in the early 1790's. Although Jefferson's refusal to dismiss Freneau shows his concern about the sources of information which should be open to the public, it does not show any intention of organizing a political party. Hamilton had, very early in the new government, set up Fenno's *Gazette of the United States* as an organ to further his views,[67] and he later gave it financial support. Under these circumstances, Jefferson did not see any reason why Freneau should be dismissed. He apparently believed in the early 1790's that if public opinion could only be informed, the measures of the government would reflect the views of its citizens. During the years 1798-1800, when Jefferson had become the leader of a full-fledged opposition party, he still put more emphasis upon newspapers and pamphlets than upon party organization. Although he did not, like Hamilton, write pamphlets and articles for newspapers, he was from an early date conscious of their importance, and by 1793 he was commenting in letters to Madison on political writings in

[67] See Thomas Denton McCormick on the elder Fenno, DAB.

a fashion which shows that he was analyzing them carefully. In fact, he seems to have been inclined to depend too much on pamphlets and newspapers. He apparently believed that public opinion would cause a change of Administration policies on vital points without there first being a change of the officers of the Administration. Had this been true—had our executive been as sensitive to public opinion as Jefferson thought— parties, the extra-constitutional organs so indispensable for representative government, would have been as unnecessary as they were generally believed to be. It was the great illusion of this period that permanent or "inveterate" parties had no place in the form of government which had been established here, and Jefferson seems to have been a man of his own time in this regard. When we see the way in which the first popular party in the United States came into being, with its roots in Committees of Correspondence like those of Revolutionary times and its forms shaped by the local institutions of the middle states, we shall see that it was a product of adjustment and growth, that it did not spring full-blown from the forehead of Jefferson or of anyone else. The Democratic party cannot be listed among Jefferson's numerous inventions.

After Jefferson assumed leadership of the party in 1797, his political strategy was less active, his personal influence in the party less important than has been generally assumed. In 1791, while he was Secretary of State, the Spanish, in an effort to strengthen themselves in Florida, offered incentives for Americans to settle there, a policy which they were to follow for decades in other of their territories adjoining ours. Jefferson was convinced that this policy would work to our advantage instead of theirs and that, if it were pursued, it would give us Florida without bloodshed. He therefore suggested to Washington that "we may complain of this seduction of our inhabitants just enough to make them believe we think it very wise policy for them, & confirm them in it."[68] Such use of an opponent's own momentum and precipitancy to destroy him is the true pattern of Jefferson's strategy in politics as well as in diplomacy. One indication that the Republican party under his leadership actually followed this strategy is to be found in a letter which he wrote Madison shortly after becoming Vice-President. The Federalists were already a war party in 1797, and a year before the XYZ Affair he saw in this fact the opportunity for the Republicans to win popular favor:

[68] Jefferson to Washington, Philadelphia, Apr. 2, 1791, Ford, *Jefferson's Works,* VI, 239.

The hope however is that as the anti-Republicans take the high ground of war, and their opponents are for everything moderate that the most moderate of those who come under contrary dispositions will join them.[69]

In politics, such a strategy as this followed directly not only from Jefferson's sense of expediency, but also from his faith in his countrymen and his conception of republican government. He wrote to Caesar Rodney in 1805, "he who would do his country the most good he can must go quietly with the prejudices of the majority until he can lead them into reason."[70] The leader of an opposition party could have no sounder precept, and it explains the conduct of Jefferson during the 1790's better than anything which has been written about him. The ultimate success of this strategy of Jefferson's was due at least as much to the views and policies of the Federalists as to any qualities of Jefferson. It would not have been so successful against opponents who had more regard for the main body of opinion in the country. But so far as Jefferson's strategy was responsible for the political triumph of his party, the credit is due to his statesmanship rather than to the qualities of management, influence, and intrigue to which it is generally attributed.

The Federalists and the writers who have supported them do not stress this aspect of Jefferson's leadership. To do so would be to focus attention upon those policies and views of government by which the Federalists lost public confidence. Instead, their explanation has laid great stress on Jefferson's personal influence. One of the best contemporary statements of this view was written by William Vans Murray:

I am inclined to *superstition,* but not to faith, and almost believe in the personal agency of the Devil. *His* influence . . . does I am convinced immense mischief in the Senate. I know several genteel men, with about as much of *science* as I have, that is, just enough to make them wonder that any mortal should have more, who I am sure are the dupes of his philosophizing dinners, in which the almost treasonable theories of universal benevolence and philanthropy blend themselves easily with the politics of the day, and are promoted by the satisfactions of the table. These are then connected, as they are unfolded over a generous glass, with the grand and enlightened views of France, with touches upon the brilliance of her *victories,* and her gorgeous strength, and the country gentleman who went well enough inclined to give a vote for plain measures of

[69] Jefferson to Madison, Philadelphia, May 18, 1797, *ibid.,* VIII, 289-90.
[70] Jefferson to Caesar Rodney, Washington, Oct. 23, 1805, Gratz Collection, PHS.

defence and preparation, gets his head turned, and comes away a philosopher, and would not for worlds interrupt such grand designs, or longer feel sentiments that evince low prejudice and narrow views.[71]

In spite of the blandishments described here, the Senate remained Federalist during the years while Jefferson presided over it. Either he did not convert many senators to his view, or they did not remain converted. As a matter of fact, Jefferson did not have, or did not use, much influence with even the Republican congressmen while he was Vice-President, as was shown by their conduct from April to July, 1798. The XYZ fever was at its highest during those months. Jefferson was convinced that the Federalists wished to get us into war with France and that if they did, they would establish a military despotism in this country. He thought that if war could be put off until the end of the session of Congress which was meeting in the spring of 1798, there would be a good chance of avoiding it. He felt that the Federalists were approaching war step by step through measures which could be defeated if the Republican members in the House would only act together. Instead, however, enough Republicans[72] went home to leave the Federalists in a majority, the Virginia members

[71] The Hague, Aug. 23, 1797, "Letters of William Vans Murray to John Quincy Adams," AHA, *Report for 1912*, 360.

[72] Madison to Jefferson, Apr. 29, 1798. ". . . I am sorry to learn that the Naval bill is likely to be carried, and particularly that any of our friends should, by their leaving Congress, be accessory to it." *Letters and Other Writings of James Madison*, 4 vols. (Congress Edition, Philadelphia, 1865), II, 138.

Same to same, May 20, 1798. ". . . It is truly to be deplored that a standing army should be let in upon us by the absence of a few sound votes." *Ibid.*, 142.

Jefferson to Madison, Philadelphia, Mar. 29, 1798. "In fact, the question of war & peace depends now on a toss of cross & pile. If we could but gain this season, we should be saved. . . ." Ford, *Jefferson's Works*, VIII, 392.

The bill for capturing French cruisers had passed the Senate and was tabled in the House. "If these bills pass and place us in a state of war, it may truly be ascribed to the desertion of our members. Of 14 who are absent 10 are from the republican side of the house had even a single one been in his place not a single one of the dangerous measures carried or to be carried would have prevailed, even the provisional army would have been rejected for it was carried but by a majority of 11." Same to same, Philadelphia, May 24, 1798, Jefferson Papers, CIV, LC. Jefferson then gave the names of absentees. His account of Republican behavior at this time as given in 1826 (Ford, *Jefferson's Works*, XII, 445-46) is at variance with the account which he gives in his letters at the time, so I have quoted more than one of the letters. The account given in the letters seems the more trustworthy in every respect. Writing in 1826, he does not give specific dates for the period to which his remarks apply. If in the latter account he refers to some period other than Apr.-Jun., 1798, it of course does not conflict with the account given in the letters quoted here.

being the worst offenders; and it was not the Republicans but the moderate Federalists who saved the country from war with France. Whether Jefferson did not attempt to rally the Republicans, or they disregarded his efforts, there is no way of knowing, but his failure to influence them on a point which he felt to be of such vital importance as this one should make us question the legend of his personal influence.

Jefferson's correspondence has been generally regarded as a great source of strength for the new party. Some writers represent him as having been almost as bewitching through his pen, at several hundred miles' distance, as Murray pictures him across his own table. Yet the political conversion of not a single important political figure can be traced to his correspondence with Jefferson; and outside Virginia, Jefferson does not appear to have had any success in his efforts to get various men, some of them stout Republicans, to take the field against the Federalists. Many of Jefferson's letters, particularly to South Carolinians, suggest that he was willing to use his personal relationships for political purposes; but Allen Jones of North Carolina, and the various Pinckneys and Rutledges, and others to whom he wrote his most persuasive letters, all remained in, or went over to, the Federalist party.[73] If there were anything which should be condemned in the writing of such letters, Jefferson could not be defended against it, for he unquestionably sought to use his personal influence for political purposes. To understand party growth in this period, however, one must realize that most of Jefferson's efforts in this direction failed. As far as we can tell now, those that he tried hardest to influence went their own way politically; those who were nearest him politically were men who happened to be so because of their own views on issues as they arose.

We cannot form a final estimate of Jefferson's personal influence upon the men he knew solely on the basis of what remains of his correspondence or from the failure of Republican congressmen to act together in the spring of 1798; but such evidence as we have does justify us in questioning

[73] An example from a letter of this type is Jefferson's to Edward Rutledge, Aug. 25, 1791. He had been writing of the evils of speculation and concluded, "Would to God, yourself General Pinckney and Major Pinckney, would come forward and aid us with your efforts. You are all known, respected, wished for; but you refuse yourselves to everything. What is to become of us, my dear friend, if the vine and fig tree withdraw, and leave us to the bramble and thorn?" Quoted in Randall, *Life of Jefferson*, II, 13. John Harold Wolfe in his *Jeffersonian Democracy in South Carolina* (Chapel Hill, 1940), 14 *n*, writes, "It is of peculiar interest that these South Carolinians and most of the others who wrote to Jefferson during the 1780's later became Federalists."

the legendary view, which will be found to rest on Federalist sources
when it rests on any. Federalist sources, of course, are of no more value
in ascertaining the purposes and organization of the Republican party
than Republican sources would be in ascertaining those of the Federalist
party. The absence of more evidence than we have upon so interesting a
subject is bound to lead to conjecture. Speculation, however, should be so
labeled; and we should remember that if we give Jefferson too large a part
in the formation of his party, we tend to overlook the political aspirations
of his generation, to obscure the state of public sentiment which Federalist
measures from 1790 on had produced, and to underrate the ability of
Republican editors, pamphleteers, and local and state leaders. These were
the errors which Jefferson's opponents made, and there is little excuse now
for repeating them.

Above all, we have been misled by attributing too much to Jefferson,
too little to his followers, humble or eminent. If Jeffersonian democracy
were as largely the creation of one man as it is sometimes represented, it
would not be democracy. The scraps of evidence we find among the letters
of Jefferson and those nearest him will throw little light on our problem
unless we view them in relation to everything that we can learn of both
of the first national parties, of the government policies of the period, and
above all, of the ideology of each of the contending groups. The development of Jeffersonian democracy is the response of the Revolutionary generation to a highly complicated set of factors; and the study of Jefferson himself, although it shows the way in which he viewed the issues, gives us
little more than the most personal aspects of his relation to this movement.

It so happens that the time of Jefferson's retirement—January, 1794,
to March, 1797—upon which the conventional treatment is perhaps the
most misleading of all, is the period on which one very careful and
scholarly work has been written. William E. Dodd's *Thomas Jeffersons
Rückkehr zur Politik 1796*[74] contains material and conclusions which
might have set us right on Jefferson's part in party organization during
these very important years, had it been more widely used. Although it was
written mainly from published sources, there is little in manuscript materials that have yet come to light which would warrant important
changes in Professor Dodd's conclusions. He placed Jefferson's decision
to accept the candidacy between May 2 and May 14, 1796, and stated that

[74] William Edward Dodd, *Thomas Jeffersons Rückkehr zur Politik 1796* (Leip-
zig, 1899).

the vote of the House of Representatives, on April 30th, to grant the money which would put the Jay Treaty into effect caused Jefferson to come to this decision.[75] He shows Jefferson's great reluctance to return to politics and the pressure which his friends put upon him to do so. His conclusions, based on a careful study of the correspondence of Jefferson and his friends, are in startling contrast to the conventional view that Jefferson spent his time in retirement organizing or directing an opposition party.

When Jefferson was about to leave Monticello for Philadelphia in 1797 to become Vice-President, he wrote to Volney:

I hope I shall see you in Georgetown, and certainly shall if the movements of the stage will permit it; for I prefer that conveyance to traveling with my own horses because it gives me what I have long been without, an opportunity of plunging into the mixed characters of my fellow-countrymen, the most useful school we can enter into and one which nothing else can supply the want of. I once intimately knew all the specimens of character which compose the aggregate mass of my fellow citizens, but age, office, & literature have too long insulated me from them. I find that either their features or my optics have considerably changed in twenty years.[76]

Many specific occasions have been suggested as the beginning of the Democratic party, such as Jefferson's return to New York from France or his first serious differences with Hamilton; but these events put too much emphasis on Jefferson. If we seek to express his true relation to the movement which he came to lead, we may find it in his boarding of the coach as he returns to public life. No physical symbol can do more than indicate the nature of a gradual development: his mounting this huge, lumbering, slow-moving vehicle, which carried people from every condition of life, presents a more accurate picture than that of his calling a powerful and mysterious party into being by his personal influence. Jefferson did not create a party: a widespread popular movement recognized and claimed him as its leader. We have now followed him to the coach; how it came to be waiting for him is a story of even greater interest and importance.

[75] *Ibid.*, 84 ff.
[76] Jefferson to Volney, Monticello, Apr. 9, 1797, Jefferson Papers, LC.

III

The Jay Treaty

1. EARLY PHASES OF THE PARTY CONFLICT

IN the preceding essays we have pointed out the dominant purpose of some of the outstanding political figures of the 1790's and the relation of each man to the more important issues of these years. We should bear in mind the stand of these men on the issues of the time, not only because they had a great deal to do with the way in which the issues were settled, but because both the men and the issues played a significant part in shaping public opinion. As important problems arose, the first question asked was how the leading figures stood upon them. Thus it would be easy to overemphasize the importance of the leaders and to picture our first political struggles merely as those of gigantic and shadowy figures. To assure balance, therefore, we must study the parties in action, where we see how they helped to shape and were in turn shaped by events. If we approach the parties from the functional point of view and can discover what they were fighting for at various times during this period, we may be somewhat less dependent than heretofore upon definitions and formulas for our understanding of them.

The relation between the party conflict and the policies which the government followed during this period shifts and varies in many respects, but it remains constant in importance and interest. Division into parties cannot be studied apart from administration policy; for it was upon such issues as our commercial policy, Funding, Assumption, the establishment of the Bank, and the ratification of Jay's treaty that some of the ablest Republican leaders went into open opposition, and it was their stand against these and other government policies which brought them most of their followers.

Until the leading measures were formulated and debated upon, until sentiment upon them had taken shape, there was no way of telling what would be the contending forces in the new government. The political leaders of this time were slow to see the necessity for political parties, but they soon saw the necessity for having public support for their policies. Party growth came in response to this need. It both increased interest in public affairs and reflected the growth of that interest from other causes. The rise of national parties, the phenomenal increase in newspaper circulation, and the number of letters carried through the mails are all evidence that horizons were widening, that men were becoming citizens of the nation instead of the state, and that everywhere their minds were being increasingly occupied by the same problems. It was the growth of parties that gave the average voter his first chance to express himself on the new questions of the day, and parties became the medium through which this awakening of public opinion influenced government policy.

The role of public opinion became greater as the decade progressed; and once the two parties took definite shape, government policy and party conflict began to resemble two unstable chemical compounds in a reversible reaction: whatever affected one affected the other. The fact that parties were only in the process of formation, that the allegiance of most of the voters was still to be won, that members kept passing from one party to the other, made the situation more rather than less complicated.

There had been parties of some permanence in almost all the states, but when and where did national parties first arise? One would naturally assume that they arose at the seat of government and that they first became evident in the House of Representatives, the branch of the government nearest the people. Orin G. Libby, an early investigator of this subject, has denied, however, that parties are to be found there at this time.[1]

Despite Libby's conclusions, there was during Washington's Presi-

[1] Orin G. Libby, "Political Factions in Washington's Administrations," *Quarterly Journal of the University of North Dakota*, III (1912), 293-303. A close investigation of the measures which Libby selected as the basis for the tabulation of his votes and an analysis of the debates upon these measures show that Libby frequently counted anti-Administration votes as pro-, and pro-Administration votes as anti-. For example, in the voting on the admission of Tennessee as a state, Libby counted the votes for the measure as pro-Administration and those against it as anti-, although the Federalists were making every effort to keep Tennessee out so that her vote would not be counted in the Presidential election of 1796. For a more detailed discussion of Libby's method of work and an explanation of the method followed here, see Joseph Charles, The Party Origins of Jeffersonian Democracy (Doctoral Dissertation, Harvard University, 1942), Appendix.

dency a progressive and rapid growth of parties which was reflected in the voting upon questions of importance in the House of Representatives. The increasing sharpness of the party division stands out most clearly if we measure it by showing the decline of no-party voting. The number of members who did not vote consistently with either party as measured by the percentage of the total in attendance fell sharply between 1790 and 1796. Selecting only those measures which were of national importance or those which members of the House felt to embody some important principle of government, we find that the no-party voting fell from 42 per cent in 1790 to 7 per cent for the Jay Treaty session, the lowest point it reached until 1798.[2] By this standard the years 1789 to 1797 would appear to be at least as important as the period from 1797 to 1801 for a study of party development.

The session table showing the number of representatives voting consistently in each party and the decreasing number of no-party voters is calculated by the voting on at least nine measures. The counting of the votes on the important measures of each session reflects a growing division in the House, but it does not show the causes for it. These causes were, of course, complex and went beyond the particular measures which were being debated in a given session. Any group of men voting on questions as they arise will discover communities and diversities of interest among themselves in the normal course of their business. When the individual no longer votes on the merits of questions as he sees them, when he thinks in terms of voting with those who have voted with him in the past or of winning support for some of his own measures which are to arise in the future, party division within the group is well on its way. If this division comes to the point where the decisions made on specific questions are secondary to the contest for power among the parties in the group, party division has reached an extreme and is furnishing motives of its own for action—which all concerned will deplore but will regard as forced upon them by their opponents.

If the nature of our problem is thus complex, it is, of course, useless to try to fix too precisely the moment at which two definite parties came into being in the House. Evidence other than that found in the party

---

[2] These are the figures if we regard voting with one party 66⅔% of the time as the test of party regularity. If to be a regular party man a member must have voted 75% of the time with one party, the figures are 54% to 14% for the same sessions. See Joseph Charles, The Party Origins of Jefferson Democracy, 215.

	I 1 Apr.-Sept. 1789			I 2 & 3 Jan.-Aug. 1790 Dec. 1790-Mar. 1791			II 1 Oct. 1791-May 1792			II 2 Nov. 1792-Mar. 1793			III 1 & 2 Dec. 1793-Jun. 1794 Nov. 1794-Mar. 1795			IV 1 Dec. 1795-Jun. 1796			IV 2 Dec. 1796-Mar. 1797			V 1 May-Jul. 1797			V 2 Nov. 1797-Jul. 1798			V 3 Dec. 1798-Mar. 1799			VI 1 Dec. 1799-May 1800			VI 2 Nov. 1800-Mar. 1801			VII 1 Dec. 1801-May 1802		
	F	R	N	F	R	N	F	R	N	F	R	N	F	R	N	F	R	N	F	R	N	F	R	N	F	R	N	F	R	N	F	R	N	F	R	N	F	R	N
New Hampshire	1	1	1	1		2	1		2	2		1	2		2	3	1		1	2	1	4			4			4			4			4			4		
Massachusetts	3	2	3	4		4	7			8			12	1	1	11	3		8	5	1	10	3		10	2	2	11	2	1	10	2	2	11	3		4	7	6
Connecticut	4		1	2		3	4			4			7			7			6		1	6	1		7			7			7			7			7		
Rhode Island		ab.		1			1			1			2			2			2			1		1	2			2			2			2			1	1	
Vermont						2				1	1		2			1	1			1	1	1	1		1	1		1	1		1	1		1	1		1	1	
New York	3	3		2	1	3	4	2		4	2		7	3		5	5		4	5	1	6	4		5	4	1	6	4		4	5	1	4	6		3	7	
New Jersey	3		1	3		1	2		2	2	1	1	4		1	2	1	1	4			4			5			4			2	3		2	3			5	
Pennsylvania	5		2	3		4	3	2	3	4	3	1	4	4	4	4	7	2	5	7	1	5	7	1	5	7		4	8	1	4	8	1	4	9		3	10	
Delaware	1			1			1						1			1			1			1			1			1			1			1			1		
Maryland	1	1	4	2		4	1	3	2	1	2	2	3	4	1	3	2	3	5	2	1	5	2	1	5	2	1	3	1	4	5	2	1	4	4		3	5	
Virginia	2	3	4	2	5	3		9	1		8	1	2	15	2		18	1	1	15	3	2	16	1	3	15	1	3	15	1	6	13		4	14	1	1	18	
N. Carolina		ab.			3	2		4	1		4	1		7	3		10			10		1	9		1	9	1	1	7	1	4	6		4	6		4	5	
S. Carolina	1	1	3	1	3	1	3	1	1	3		2	1		4	2	4		2	2		3	3		3	3		3	2		5	1		3	2	1	3	2	
Georgia	1		2		3		1	2			2	1		2			2			2			2			2			1			2			1			1	
Kentucky											2			2			2		1	1			2			2			2			2			1			1	
Tennessee																				1						1			1			1			1			1	
	25	11	21	22	15	27	28	23	14	29	25	11	45	38	20	40	57	7	36	55	12	49	50	4	51	48	6	50	44	8	55	46	5	51	52	2	38	64	0

F = Federalist   R = Republican   N = No-Party

    The basis for the tabulation of the first three Congresses is to be found in Joseph Charles, *The Party Origins of Jeffersonian Democracy* (Doctoral Dissertation, Harvard University, 1942), Appendix. The balance of the table is based on computations from Manning J. Dauer, *The Adams Federalists*, (Baltimore, 1953), Appendix III, used in dissertation form by Joseph Charles with permission of the author.

voting fixes the time when the Republicans first felt themselves in a position to offer a program of their own instead of remaining on the defensive. The program was expressed in Madison's resolutions on Jefferson's Commercial Report; and the date, January, 1794, immediately after Jefferson's retirement, may serve as the dividing point between the two earliest phases of the growth of the Republicans in the House of Representatives.

While Jefferson referred to the Republican party in letters as early as 1792, there is no reliable evidence that he was actively engaged that early in organizing a popular party, or indeed that what he spoke of as the Republican party existed. He probably used the term to prevent the Federalists from labeling all opposition to Hamilton's measures as anti-Federalism. The Republicans in the House of Representatives at this time had only two members from New England, one each from Vermont and Massachusetts; and their scattered Pennsylvania and New York members included no particularly active or able men. We might very well call Jefferson's "Republican" party at this time a group of Virginia representatives who picked up any support they could from the members of other delegations.[3]

What success this group had in the first sessions of Congress was limited largely to measures in which the issue was one of abstract republicanism.[4] They could usually get the support of the neutral members in limiting the executive powers and combating the threat of Cabinet government, but they failed to hold it on the vital questions of government finance.

Yet it was by their stand on finance that the Republicans hoped to win public support, and considerations of that issue dominated their own think-

[3] These conclusions were drawn from a careful study of the debates and the votes on the most important issues for the years indicated, *Annals of Congress* (Washington, 1834-56).

[4] Examples might include the following: a measure to have "all writs or processes, issuing out of the Supreme or Circuit courts" written in the name of the United States instead of "the President thereof" (carried 28 to 22); defeat of a Senate amendment giving the President the right to apply an appropriation for salaries of foreign service officers as he saw fit, instead of specific salaries as the House had originally written the bill (defeated 38 to 18); refusal of the House to allow the Postmaster General the right to establish cross post roads; defeat of a Senate amendment to the coinage bill which would have put the President's head on our coins; and finally, defeat of a Senate amendment to an appropriation bill by which the army appropriation would not have been itemized. In that order: *ibid.*, Sept. 25, 1789; May 27, 1790; Jul. 22, 1790; Mar. 24, 1792; Feb. 22, 1793.

ing on political subjects. They soon came to regard Hamilton's system as having been designed to strip them of the "power of the purse" and to prevent them from exercising control or restraint over the Administration. One of the speeches of John F. Mercer of Maryland shows how the issue of the public debt was woven into Republican ideology.[5] Mercer maintained that the fact that we could not rightly bind another generation financially was ". . . as demonstrable as any proposition in Euclid." He stated that we should accumulate no debt which could not be paid off in twenty years. For to pass this line would destroy

. . . that great principle which alone was the cause of the war with Great Britain. . . . That taxation and representation should go hand in hand. We have no one quality of the Representatives of posterity—not elected by them, and not responsible to them. . . . It destroys one great check of free legislation—that the legislator should feel, in his own property, the burden of the tax he lays, and the contract he makes for society. It avoids that still greater check, that the constituents should feel the burdens their Representatives impose. The people never act but from feelings: so long, therefore, as their deputies contract for and at the expense of posterity, they act in perfect safety.

If we consider the long-run political effects of Hamilton's program and the public feeling which could have been stirred up against it at the time it was proposed, perhaps the most extraordinary thing about these measures is that they did not serve as the immediate basis for an effective opposition party. The reason is that the Republican party, like the Federalist, was made up of both former opponents and former supporters of the Constitution, and anti-Federalism was at no time their dominating principle. The leading Republicans were in favor of the Constitution, particularly after the amendments to it, and were willing to make almost any sacrifice to give the new government a fair start. Madison, for example, who had opposed both Funding and Assumption, voted for the Excise Bill. By the time this bill was offered, a large debt had been funded, and the cost of meeting it and other national expenses had to be paid if the new government was to succeed. During these years Madison showed a willingness to vote for almost any measure which would raise revenue.[6] Once Funding and Assumption were adopted, no opposition could be made to the steps necessary to pay the bill without threatening the existence of

[5] *Ibid.*, Mar. 30, 1792, 504-05, *passim.*
[6] See his votes on revenue measures in *Annals of Congress.*

the new government. The basic measures of Hamilton's economic system were not, in 1790-91, a suitable target for a party which did not wish to weaken the new government or to endanger national unity.

Even after Jefferson had come to the conclusion that the success of Hamilton's plans was incompatible with the continued existence of a representative government, he for some years played little if any part in the creation of a popular national party. From the time when he and Hamilton became open antagonists in the spring of 1792 until he left the Cabinet, Jefferson's influence upon the opposition party seems to have been largely a negative one. He endeavored to persuade Washington that the opposition were not anti-Federalists, disorganizers, and Jacobins, as they were usually called;[7] and there are indications that he tried to get the party to avoid giving grounds for such charges. He wrote to Madison of the contested election between Clinton and Jay for the governorship of New York, at the time when the Republicans were considering supporting the former as Vice-President in 1792:

It does not seem possible to defend Clinton as a just or disinterested man if he does not decline the Office, of which there is no symptom; and I really apprehend that the cause of republicanism will suffer and its votaries be thrown into schism by embarking it in support of this man, and for what? to draw over the antifederalists who are not numerous enough to be worth drawing over.[8]

Until after Jefferson left the Cabinet at the end of 1793, the Republican members of Congress did little except try to prevent the passing of measures they regarded as harmful. It was in the following January that they took the offensive and attempted to win a large bloc of the Federalists' New England support away from them. The program with which Madison began the first strategic moves against the Federalists was not one which could be called anti-Federalist, particularist, or States' rights. It was based upon a strong and generally shared national sentiment, hatred of the British Navigation Acts and the commercial monopoly which had been erected upon them. Madison offered resolutions providing for higher duties upon the manufactured goods and the shipping of those nations

[7] Jefferson to Washington, Philadelphia, May 23, 1792, Paul Leicester Ford, ed., *The Works of Thomas Jefferson,* 12 vols. (New York and London, 1904-05), VI, 487 ff. Hereafter, Jefferson, *Works.*

[8] Jefferson to Madison, Jun. 21, 1792, *ibid.,* 123-24.

with whom we had no commercial treaties. The resolutions were based upon Jefferson's "Report on the Privileges and Restrictions on the Commerce of the United States in Foreign Countries,"[9] which he had submitted to the House before resigning from the Cabinet. The report showed that Great Britain was the only country with whom we had extensive trade who would not make a commercial treaty, and Madison's resolutions were designed to win commercial favors from her by putting a higher duty upon her goods and shipping than there was upon those of the countries who gave us commercial privileges. Madison stated that the purpose of his resolutions was to realize more fully that commercial independence which he had understood to be one of the main objects of the Constitution.

Against the background of general hostility to Britain because of her commercial policies since 1783,[10] the early debates of the new government are of particular interest. The question of our future commercial policy was the first serious matter to be taken up when Congress met in New York in 1789. To the great amazement of some of the staunchest supporters of the Constitution, it became apparent that there was a strong group opposed to any discrimination against the countries, including Great Britain, which were not in treaty with us. This group was successful when the question first arose in the summer of 1789, and their success has been laid to the influence of Washington and Hamilton,[11] though Washington has recorded that he went contrary to his own judgment on this point.[12]

[9] *Ibid.,* 98 ff.

[10] The commercial policy adopted by Great Britain toward the United States after the Revolution was apparently dictated by political circumstances in the House of Commons. See Helen Taft Manning, *British Colonial Government after the American Revolution, 1782-1820* (New Haven and London, 1933), 40. For protest of West Indies see *ibid.,* 42-43. Prices rose as high as 100% on the Islands when trade with the United States was stopped in 1783. See also *ibid.,* 10-12, for general importance of American trade to Great Britain, 1783-1800.

[11] After seeing the correspondence of Washington with Gouverneur Morris, who was then at the court of Great Britain, William Maclay wrote, "From the letters from the President it appears that the vote against discrimination which had involved us in difficulties with France was the work of the President, avowedly procured by his influence; and that he did it to facilitate a connection with Great Britain, thus offering direct offense to France and incurring the contempt of Great Britain, for she has spurned every overture made to her." Edgar Stanton Maclay, ed., *Journal of William Maclay* (New York, 1890), 392. See also 96-97.

[12] Washington gave the following explanation of his conduct with regard to the bill providing for commercial discrimination in his letter to David Stuart, New York, Jul. 26, 1789: "The opposition of the Senate to the discrimination in the Tonnage Bill, was so adverse to my ideas of justice and policy, that, I should have suffered it to pass into a Law without my signature, had I not been assured by some members

According to Madison's letter to Jefferson of June 30, 1789, the Federalists in opposing commercial discrimination were taking their first step away from the nationalism of their earlier views. It is not possible even now to say with certainty why they did so, but it would appear from earlier letters of John Adams, and from those of Madison and Washington written at the time, that Hamilton's policy of giving Britain the most-favored-nation status while she gave nothing in return marked a definite break with earlier Federalist views.[13]

According to Monroe,[14] Madison's presentation of his resolutions January 3, 1794, which revived the issue of discrimination, was an attempt to give the Republican party a national foundation. The Republicans regarded his resolutions as an effort to regulate commerce with an eye to the economic interests of every section. They were in particular a bid for New England support, and they came at a time when that region, as well as the rest of the country, was in the first flush of its enthusiasm for the French Revolution. They came also when the shipping interests were feeling the first impact of large-scale confiscation of their ships by the British. By 1793 France very much needed supplies from the United States, and she presented such a market for our produce as never before. She also opened her West Indian islands to our shipping, and since we followed the policy of repaying our debt to her by letting her purchase

---

of that body, that they were preparing another Bill which would answer the purpose more effectually without being liable to the objections, and to the consequences which they *feared* would have attended the discrimination which was proposed in the Tonnage Law." J. C. Fitzpatrick, ed., *The Writings of George Washington from the Original Manuscript Sources, 1777-1805*, 39 vols. (Washington, 1931-44), XXX, 363. Hereafter, Fitzpatrick, *Washington's Writings.*

[13] *Letters and Other Writings of James Madison*, 4 vols. (Congress Edition, Philadelphia, 1865), I, 480-83. John Adams to Sam Adams, Jan. 26, 1786, New York Public Library (hereafter, NYPL) *Bulletin,* X (1906), 24; Jun. 2, 1786, *ibid.,* 242-43. Reference from Manning J. Dauer, *The Adams Federalists* (Baltimore, 1953), 78.

[14] Monroe to Jefferson, Philadelphia, Mar. 3, 1794, Jefferson Papers, Library of Congress (hereafter, LC). "You were aware of the motive in commencing the session by some act connected with the present state of our affairs, founded on the publick sentiment, and which should at the same time vindicate our rights & interests and likewise shun possible pretexts for war on the part of the power it was meant to affect, and the propositions introduced by Mr. Madison were tho't best calculated to accomplish this object. . . . An opposition to our carrying trade by their [the commercial states'] own members will affect them in such a manner, they will all know the fact & understand the motives. I therefore hope for the best from the discussion of these propositions and think symptoms to the Eastward authorize the expectation it will be verified."

supplies in this country with funds furnished by our government, British captures alone stood in the way of a great increase in our trade with her. Our business with Great Britain continued to increase also, as the French blockade was not so effective as the British one, and trade with Great Britain was still much greater than that with any other country. We sold her more than nine million dollars worth of goods and bought from her fifteen million.[15]

Great Britain's capture of our ships and her system of commercial monopoly were not our only grievances. She still held our western posts and was becoming increasingly threatening in that direction. On February 10, 1794, Lord Dorchester, Governor-General of Canada, made a highly inflammatory speech to the western Indians, one which was regarded by many Americans as a direct challenge to war.[16] Thus in the early months of 1794 the Revolutionary generation looked out upon a familiar scene. No matter which way they turned, it seemed to them that the British stood in their path. Many Americans had been outraged by the behavior of Citizen Genêt, and the conduct of France was in some respects indefensible; but there was a difference between the provocations of France and those of Great Britain. The former were a blow, but the latter were a blow upon an old wound.[17]

[15] Jefferson's "Report on the Privileges and Restrictions on the Commerce of the United States in Foreign Countries," Jefferson, *Writings,* VI, 98 ff. The table from which the figures quoted are taken is on pp. 100-01.

[16] Evidence that feeling ran high against the British early in 1794 is found in at least two of Henry Van Schaack's letters to Theodore Sedgwick: Kinderhook, N. Y., Mar. 20, 1794, "Let me repeat that I believe Oswego and the little posts above and below the Falls of Niagra [*sic*] will be taken by our western citizens if in this session of Congress something effectually is not done. I rely much on the information that is now handed about." Sedgwick Papers, Massachusetts Historical Society (hereafter, MHS). Also Mar. 23, 1794, "Last Mondays paper confirms me more that there is a concerted plan to have hostilities committed independent of government." *Ibid.*

[17] The question of the relative damage inflicted upon our shipping by France and Britain during the 1790's is an extraordinarily difficult one, and appears to have been treated in a purely partisan manner at the time. Mr. Monaghan probably states the conventional view of present-day historians when he writes, "French depredations against American commerce were far greater than any ever committed by Great Britain." Frank Monaghan, *John Jay* (New York and Indianapolis, 1935), 412. No conclusive judgment on this point is given in Anna Cornelia Clauder, *American Commerce as Affected by the Wars of the French Revolution and Napoleon, 1793-1812* (Philadelphia, 1932). The only place where materials have been given which would permit the forming of even a tentative judgment on the relative damage inflicted on our shipping by France and Britain during the 1790's, appears to be in Samuel Flagg Bemis, *A Diplomatic History of the United States* (New York, 1936),

Madison's resolutions, which had in the beginning been favored by the feeling against Great Britain, were put aside as that feeling became stronger and as people demanded more immediate and drastic steps than the resolutions provided. Between March and June of 1794 several measures were urged, and some of them passed, which went farther than any Madison had suggested. Congress empowered the President to lay a complete embargo on our shipping for six months. Jonathan Dayton moved a sequestration of British debts, with at least a part of the money we owed to be used in compensating our citizens for their losses by British seizures. A Non-Intercourse Bill was passed. It should be observed, however, that all these were emergency measures, which went beyond anything Madison had contemplated but which would leave our commercial relations, once the measures should be removed, precisely as they had been before. The Non-Intercourse Bill passed, fifty-eight to thirty-eight, with the New Jersey and Pennsylvania delegations voting largely with the South,[18]—an alignment which, if it should persist, would be fatal to the Federalists. The measure sanctioned by this bill was defeated in the Senate, though only by the casting vote of John Adams, on the grounds that it would be harmful to the negotiations of the special envoy whom it had been decided to send to Great Britain.

Madison's resolutions were sidetracked, and it might appear that they had no particular political significance. Usually very little attention is given them in tracing the development of the two political parties. Yet because of their part in helping to set the stage for the Jay Treaty, they mark one of the milestones in the growth of parties. The debates on them brought the Republicans such a measure of support from the Middle states and New England as to convince the Federalists that the whole dangerous question of our commercial relations had to be taken out of the hands of the House of Representatives, where their party faced certain defeat, and put under the control of the Cabinet and Senate by being made the object of a special mission and a new treaty. Thus the first aggressive maneuver of the Republicans had great, if wholly unexpected, results. To the extent that the Federalists were moved by this consideration, the Jay Treaty,

---

114-15, and 114 *n* (Court of Claims data). See also Timothy Pickering to Edward Stevens, Trenton, Sept. 5, 1800, Pickering Papers, XII, 10-12, MHS; Liston to Grenville, New York, Oct. 18, 1800, British State Papers (transcripts), LC; and Benjamin Goodhue to Fisher Ames, Dec. 20, 1800, and Mar. 20, 1801, Ames MSS., Dedham Historical Society.

[18] *Annals of Congress,* Apr. 21, 1794.

the most important measure in its political effects between the institution of Hamilton's financial program and the election of 1800, stemmed directly from the conditions of the party conflict in the early months of 1794.

Jefferson wrote of Jay's treaty in September, 1795:

A bolder party-stroke was never struck. For it certainly is an attempt of a party, which finds they have lost their majority in one branch of the legislature, to make a law by the aid of the other branch & of the executive, under color of a treaty, which shall bind up the hands of the adverse branch from ever restraining the commerce of their patron-nation.[19]

A study of the correspondence of the most eminent Federalists during the spring of 1794,[20] while they were planning to get a special envoy sent to England, would indicate that the judgment of Jefferson as to the origins of this treaty was a sound one, though the motive of most of these men was not pro-British, as he represented it. Above all, the sending of the mission was an effort to prevent the "mischievous measures" which Hamil-

[19] Jefferson to Madison, Sept. 21, 1795, Jefferson, *Writings*, VIII, 193. As to the actual inception of the treaty, Ralston Hayden says, "Probably the outstanding point in connection with the negotiation of the treaty, however, is the extent to which a small group of Federalist Senators, who were also among Washington's most trusted advisers, dominated the entire proceeding. These men suggested the mission; they secured its acceptance by the President, and practically directed the selection of the envoy; they secured his confirmation by the Senate; they sent him out fully cognizant with their views as to what sort of a treaty should be striven for and under very flexible instructions from the Department of State.

"It is also important to remember that this group prevailed upon the Senate to approve the general purpose of the mission by confirming the nomination of the envoy without demanding to be informed of and to pass judgment upon the particular instructions under which the negotiation was to be carried on." Joseph Ralston Hayden, *The Senate and Treaties, 1789-1817* (New York and London, 1920), 92.

[20] King kept a record of the events leading up to the sending of Jay, beginning on Mar. 10, 1794 (Charles R. King, ed., *The Life and Correspondence of Rufus King,* 6 vols. [New York, 1894-1900; hereafter, King, *Correspondence*], I, 517 ff.), all of which should be read by anyone interested in the circumstances which gave rise to the mission. On Apr. 17, he recorded that Jay told the President that the resolutions (Madison's) were in the nature of a menace and that Great Britain would and ought to refuse to treat with us if they were adopted. The comments of King, of Wolcott and his correspondents (George Gibbs, ed., *Memoirs of the Administrations of Washington and John Adams,* 2 vols. [New York, 1846; hereafter, Gibbs, *Memoirs*], I, 117 ff.), of Hamilton in particular (John Church Hamilton, ed., *The Works of Alexander Hamilton,* 7 vols. [New York, 1850-51; hereafter, Hamilton, *Works*], IV, 564), and of Sedgwick (Sedgwick Papers, Jan.-May, 1794, MHS), would seem to support the view that the origin and main object of the Jay mission lay in the party conflict, though none of these men specifically affirmed it.

ton spoke of at the time,[21] a counterattack to defeat the Republican maneuver which had given that party a majority. As this majority was increased in the election of 1794,[22] giving the Republicans the only strongly
Republican House they had between 1789 and 1800, the dependence of the
Federalists upon the success of Jay's treaty grew greater. Their continued
control of the government came to hang upon its adoption.

2. THE JAY TREATY

As we have seen, Jay was sent to Great Britain not only because of the
strained relations between that country and the United States, which is
the reason usually given for his mission, but also because of the party
struggle and the condition of public opinion in this country. In order to
understand the prolonged and bitter fight over the adoption of the Jay
Treaty, it is necessary to keep in mind each of these factors in its immediate background: the one which grew out of the international situation
and the one which sprang from domestic politics. Viewing only the relative situations of the two countries, the terms which Jay brought back may
have been as good as we could have expected, as defenders of the Treaty
have always maintained. The opposition, however, as well as many who
had previously been strong Federalists, did not believe them to be, and the
conditions of the Treaty put more powerful weapons into the hands of
the Republicans for the struggle against it than any of them had expected
beforehand. The party struggle had gone far enough that there would
probably have been at least a perfunctory opposition to almost any treaty
that could have been drawn up between the two countries in 1794, but
only the conditions of the Jay Treaty itself could have brought about such
widespread popular opposition as occurred. We must then, before plunging into the fight over the Treaty, examine its terms briefly.

Since Madison's proposal of the commercial resolutions directed against
Great Britain had been of importance in bringing about the Treaty, it
is interesting to note that all such regulation of British commerce and

[21] Hamilton, *Works,* IV, 564.

[22] "Thus the entire Sea Coast area, which had been the Federal backbone in 1788,
showed signs of Federal disintegration in 1794. This transition to Republicanism was
permanent, although in certain places it met with a temporary check in the elections
of 1796 and 1798." George Daniel Luetscher, *Early Political Machinery in the United
States* (Philadelphia, 1903), 59 *n.* Luetscher's conclusion as to the long-run significance of Republican gains in the Congressional election of 1794 may not be sound,
but there is no doubt that these gains were very disturbing to the Federalists at that
time.

shipping to our shores as his resolutions proposed was barred under the Treaty. Although Jay obtained no commercial privileges except trade with the West Indies, and that on conditions so stringent that we refused to accept that part of the Treaty, we gave up for ten years the right to impose any tonnage or tariff discrimination upon British ships or goods.[23] Thus such questions as those raised by Madison's resolutions, which had afforded a strategic rallying point for Republicans, could no longer vex the Federalists once the Treaty was ratified. As far as trade with Great Britain was concerned, we were left in the same position that we had thought so intolerable under the Confederation. Other weaknesses of the Treaty, as evaluated by Samuel Flagg Bemis, include Jay's failure to maintain the honor of the Federal courts in the matter of debts owed to British citizens, which were now to be determined by a mixed commission; the lack of a provision to secure recognition of our adopted principles of international maritime law; the absence of an article protecting our seamen from impressment; and, finally, the failure to secure a mutual hands-off policy with regard to Indians in each other's territory.[24]

It would appear that this treaty could be defended, from the American point of view, only upon the assumptions which underlie "Admiral Mahan's statement that the signature by England of any treaty at all with the United States at that time was an event of 'epochal significance,' a recognition of the existence of American nationality of far greater import than the technical recognition of independence forced from George III in 1783."[25] This was not, however, the view which most Americans of that time took of the matter. They were not asking for recognition of the existence of American nationality. They were asking for a removal of grievances, some of which impaired our sovereignty, and for a basis of commercial and diplomatic relationship which would enable us to remain at peace with her without becoming a British satellite.

A deep and general aversion to the terms of the Jay Treaty is apparent throughout the whole effort to get it approved. As Gaillard Hunt says, "Washington did not pretend to like the treaty. After Jay had delivered it he kept it for four months before he could bring himself to submit it to the Senate."[26] When it was finally submitted, it was passed, after prolonged discussion, on June 24, 1795, by the minimum number of votes

[23] Samuel Flagg Bemis, *Jay's Treaty* (New York, 1923), 257.
[24] *Ibid.*, 259-61.
[25] *Ibid.*, 269-70.
[26] Gaillard Hunt, Introduction to Bemis, *Jay's Treaty*, xiii.

necessary. Senator Mason of Virginia, in violation of the resolution of complete secrecy passed by the Senate when consideration of the Treaty began, gave a copy of it to Benjamin Franklin Bache, editor of the *Aurora*,[27] who printed it on June 29 and personally carried the news to Boston, scattering copies of the Treaty at all his stops along the way. Washington had expected to sign the Treaty if the Senate recommended it, but hesitated as the feeling against it began to mount. At the same time the Administration learned that the British had issued a new order for the seizure of our ships carrying provisions to France, an order mistakenly regarded at that time as a renewal of their provision order of June, 1793.[28] Britain continued to retain our posts, the surrender of which was to be our one tangible benefit from the Treaty, until we should ratify,

[27] Mason has been accused of most unworthy motives in revealing the terms of the Treaty to the public. Howard Crosby Rice suggests that Mason got 500 guineas or $2,333 through James Swan from the French government for making the terms of the Treaty known. "James Swan: Agent of the French Republic, 1794-96," *New England Quarterly*, X (Sept., 1937), 481. Thomas Perkins Abernethy in his article on Mason in Allen Johnson and Dumas Malone, eds., *Dictionary of American Biography* (New York, 1928-44), says that his motives were undoubtedly honorable. Madison wrote to Monroe, Philadelphia, Dec. 20, 1795, "The Senate, after a few weeks consultation, ratified the Treaty as you have seen. The injunction of secrecy was then dissolved by a full House, and quickly after restored sub modo, in a thin one. Mr. Mason disregarding the latter vote sent the Treaty to the press. . . ." Gaillard Hunt, ed., *The Writings of James Madison*, 9 vols. (New York, 1900-10), VI, 258. As a matter of fact, for some time various senators and other officials had been telling friends and relatives a part at least of what was in the Treaty. Gibbs, *Memoirs*, I, 199-202. Mason, in a letter which he gave Bache to print with the Treaty, claimed that he was giving it to the public to correct the impressions formed by garbled and incorrect versions that were floating about. Moncure Daniel Conway, *Omitted Chapters of History Disclosed in the Life and Papers of Edmund Randolph* (New York and London, 1888), 295. Hereafter, Conway, *Randolph*. According to Randolph, Washington gave him a copy of the Treaty to be published on the day it appeared. *Ibid.*, 261. Hammond wrote to Grenville, Jun. 5, 1795, "To be sure the proceedings of the Treaty have been secret, but your Lordship may be assured of the authenticity of the circumstances I have mentioned, as they were last night communicated to me in confidence by Mr. Wolcott, the present Secretary of the Treasury." British State Papers (transcripts), NYPL.

[28] Josiah Turner Newcomb states that this was not a renewal of the provision order, seizures under which were contrary to Jay's treaty. ". . . there had been a complete shift in the legal basis for the seizures, for the British were now relying on the right to seize enemy property, in neutral bottoms, a course of action the legality of which in proved cases was sanctioned in the treaty and could not be denied under international law." "New Light on Jay's Treaty," *American Journal of International Law*, XXVIII (Oct., 1934), 687. Newcomb shows, however, that all Americans at the time believed that England was going contrary to the provisions of the newly concluded Treaty, and that it was ratified by us while under that impression.

and the new order for the seizure of our ships was regarded as a further attempt at coercion on her part. According to Randolph, Washington told him on July 13 that he "might have informed Mr. Hammond that he [Washington] would never ratify if the provision-order was not removed out of the way."[29] Of Washington's Cabinet, Randolph alone opposed ratification before the order should be rescinded, though Wolcott wished us to ratify without communicating the fact that we had done so until the order was removed.[30]

While the question was in this state, Washington left for Mount Vernon to deliberate further on the matter. Fearful that if the Treaty were ratified, it would so divide the country as to give the French every opportunity to cause embarrassment to our government, he considered that there was more to be apprehended, whether the Treaty was signed or not, "than from any other crisis since the beginning of the government."[31] The inner circle of the Federalist party fairly held its breath, awaiting Washington's decision. Oliver Ellsworth wrote cryptically, "If the President decides wrong, or does not decide *soon, his good fortune will forsake him.*"[32] Noah Webster wrote to Oliver Wolcott, "The peace of our Country stands almost committed in either event. . . . A rejection sacrifices Mr. Jay & perhaps many of his friends, a ratification threatens the popularity of the President, whose personal influence is now more essential than ever to our Union."[33] Christopher Gore wrote to King that Washington's delay in signing the Treaty was doing the government incalculable harm in New England:

Of all the critical situations in which the government has been placed, this is the most extreme. . . . I know of but one step that can arrest this mania, that affords any hope of supporting the government. An address from the President to the people of the United States, stating that he had ratified the treaty. . . .[34]

[29] Conway, *Randolph,* 267.

[30] Wolcott to Hamilton, Aug. 10, Aug. 15, 1795, Hamilton Papers, LC.

[31] Washington to Randolph, Mt. Vernon, Jul. 29, 1795, Gratz Collection, Pennsylvania Historical Society (hereafter, PHS).

[32] William Garrett Brown, *The Life of Oliver Ellsworth* (New York and London, 1905), 220.

[33] Webster to Wolcott, Jul. 30, 1795, Emily Ellsworth Ford Skeel, ed., and Emily Ellsworth Fowler Ford, comp., *Notes on the Life of Noah Webster,* 2 vols. (New York, 1912), I, 393.

[34] Aug. 14, 1795, King, *Correspondence,* II, 23. Gore urged that King and Hamilton induce the President to act decisively in favor of the Treaty.

When in 1791 Washington had hesitated and taken his full ten days before signing the Bank Bill, the Republicans claimed that the Federalists became very impatient and even threatening.[35] In 1795 Federalist sources show that there would probably have been a split in the party had Washington failed them. Stephen Higginson wrote that if the Treaty were not ratified, "The President and Senate will be at open points, with Jay & Hamilton &c on the side of the latter."[36] We have no evidence that intimations of this sort reached Washington, and that they did seems highly improbable. Such threats would not have influenced him. What is significant is that during this period when the Republicans were most active in stirring up public opinion, the Federalists were comparatively quiet. Until they had obtained Washington's approval, they had little basis for an appeal to the public.

While the country was completely absorbed in the question of what Washington would do, Hammond, the British minister, showed Wolcott a dispatch written by Fauchet, the former French minister to the United States, which had been taken in March of that year when the corvette *Jean Bart* was captured by the British man-of-war *Cerberus*. The dispatch contained an account dated October 24, 1794, which stated that Randolph, the Secretary of State, had approached Fauchet at that time and had asked him for a sum of money with which he could insure the loyalty of three or four men whose conduct was believed to be of vital importance to the Republicans and hence to France.[37] Upon news that a very urgent matter required his immediate presence, Washington left Mount Vernon and returned to Philadelphia on August 11. On the following day he saw the dispatch and said that he would ratify the Treaty. Randolph, from whom all news of this had been kept, was sent to tell Hammond, with whom he was not on good terms, that we would ratify the Treaty. When the dispatch was shown to Randolph in the presence of the Cabinet, he resigned and the Treaty was ratified. In the controversy which followed

[35] See Henry Stephens Randall, *The Life of Thomas Jefferson*, 3 vols. (New York, 1858), I, 631, for account of Madison's remarks on Washington's aversion to the Bank Bill and the Jay Treaty.

[36] Higginson to Pickering, Boston, Aug. 16, 1795, Pickering Papers, XX, 32, MHS.

[37] The best of the Federalist sources for the account of Randolph's disgrace is Gibbs, *Memoirs*, I, 232 ff., though the preceding pages should also be read to form an estimate of Randolph's importance in the struggle over the Treaty. [*Editor's note:* See Irving Brant, "Edmund Randolph Not Guilty," *William and Mary Quarterly*, 3d ser., VII (April, 1950), 179-98.]

Randolph's attempt at self-vindication,[38] he and those Republicans who embraced his cause sought to prove that the accusations against him were merely part of a maneuver to get the Treaty accepted and that Randolph had been disgraced because he was the one Cabinet member who was not in favor of immediate and unqualified acceptance of the Treaty as passed by the Senate. In answer, Washington maintained that the charges against Randolph had had nothing to do with his decision to sign the Treaty.

It seems probable that the Republicans weakened their hold upon the public and their position with regard to the Treaty to the extent that they embraced Randolph's side of the dispute. Many Republicans thought that Washington had lost all his influence and popularity by signing the Treaty, but no matter how great his losses in this respect, few people were willing to hear him attacked in the terms which Randolph and his adherents used. In one letter Randolph said that Washington had shown toward him "treachery unexampled since Tiberius," and such charges as this only placed Randolph in a worse light than before. It seems clear that whatever motives lay behind his "exposure" and disgrace, the incident was highly effective in diverting attention from questions relating directly to the Treaty, where the Republicans stood on comparatively firm ground with regard to the public opinion of the time, to a contest largely personal in nature.

While the events related above were taking place, the attention of the American people from Georgia to New Hampshire was engrossed as never before in a practical decision of government. Should we or should we not ratify the Treaty? The Republicans had taken the initiative with petitions, incendiary pamphlets, and a series of public meetings held in the larger cities, each of which addressed a memorial to the President. The Federalists denounced those who attended these meetings as the scum of society; but if it was the scum of society which showed this degree of interest—for some of the meetings were large—Jay's treaty is all the more noteworthy as a lesson in the political education of the public during this decade. John Beckley, who had taken a leading part in the planning of these meetings all over the country, wrote of the one in Philadelphia:

On Saturday, a memorial to the President will be presented, which if adopted will be carried through the different wards of the city and offered for the

[38] Edmund Randolph, *A Vindication of Mr. Randolph's Resignation* (Philadelphia, 1795).

signature of the individual citizens, by which means we shall discover the names and numbers of the British adherents, old Tories and Aristocrats who modestly assume the title of Federalists, and stile themselves *the best* friends of our beloved President. At the same time it will effectually show the major and decided sense of the great commercial city of Philadelphia. Is it not a painful reflection, my friend, that the machinations and intrigues of a British faction in our country, should place our good old president in the distressing situation of singly opposing himself to the almost unanimous voice of his fellow citizens, and endangering the peace, happiness, and union of America, as well as destroying his own tranquillity, peace of mind, good name, and fame. But I trust in heaven to enlighten his mind and give him wisdom and firmness to turn away the evil cup so insidiously prepared for him.[39]

Once the President had signed the Treaty, the real contest over it began, as the Republicans were determined to block the appropriation which the House of Representatives had to make in order to carry into effect certain provisions of the Treaty. After the President's signature, Beckley and his associates made a second attempt to whip up general public feeling, or at least to prevent its decline. To DeWitt Clinton, Beckley wrote:

We perfectly accord with you in sentiment, and are adopting measures on our part in furtherance of your ideas. A change in the public sentiment now so universally manifested against the treaty, is the great desideratum of our opponents, as they mean to influence a majority of the Representatives in its favor at the coming meeting of Congress;—to this object all their efforts will be pointed, and to frustrate them we have concluded an address to the people of the United States to be printed and dispersed in handbills in the same mode and subject to the same rules of secrecy that we observed in the case of the petition, respecting which not a suspicion is yet excited here—By this means, we hope to give the first effectual blow and to make it as impressive as possible, we shall incorporate in it . . . a history of the late intrigues in the Cabinet, connected with the causes of Mr. Randolph's resignation, which produced the President's ratification of the treaty, and a revocation of his first determination officially made known to Hammonds [*sic*] not to ratify. . . . Rely on every effort and cooperation here in pursuit of what we religiously think our country's political salvation rests on—the defeat of the treaty.[40]

Although public interest in the Treaty did not remain during the

[39] John Beckley to DeWitt Clinton, Philadelphia, Jul. 24, 1795, DeWitt Clinton Papers, Columbia University Library (hereafter, CUL).
[40] Same to same, Philadelphia, Sept. 3, 1795, *ibid*.

winter of 1795-96 at the level it had reached during the previous summer and fall, it soon revived. In March the question was brought before the House of Representatives of an appropriation to put the Treaty into effect. The parties fought now not only over the merits of the Treaty, but also over the question whether the House had the power under the Constitution to refuse to appropriate the money necessary for a treaty already ratified by the President and the Senate. Thus the passing of the Treaty had again come to depend largely upon extraneous factors. The Constitutional issue presented a true dilemma. Either the Senate did not have complete power as to treaties, or the House complete power to initiate financial measures, both of which powers had been generally assumed supreme.

The immediate effect of this apparent conflict of jurisdiction was to win some support for the Federalists from those who thought that the House was moved by jealousy of its powers or by mere political obstructionism, and who regarded its conduct as another example of the viciousness of party spirit. To many Republican representatives it must have appeared that the practical question for them to decide was whether it was best to defeat the Treaty and destroy the prestige of the House, or to pass the Treaty, vindicate their party and body as moderate and magnanimous, and hope thereby to prevent disaster to Republicanism later. Aaron Kitchell, a Republican representative from New Jersey who regarded the Jay Treaty as part of an effort to prepare the minds of the people for a rupture with France, nevertheless voted for it so that whatever evils followed could not then be laid on the House of Representatives. "Should this be the case it would exactly answer the wish of those who are wishing to destroy the check which the House of Representatives have in the government."[41]

When the House voted to ask Washington for the papers which would explain the negotiations on the Treaty, his negative reply, instructing the House to limit its concern with treaties to appropriations,[42] must have been very galling to Madison and other Republicans who knew at least as much as Washington of the view which the Federal Convention took on this and other matters. On the other hand, it seems to have strengthened the Federalist position in the country at large.[43]

[41] Aaron Kitchell to Ebenezer Elmer, Philadelphia, Mar. 31, 1796, PHS.

[42] Mar. 30, 1796, Fitzpatrick, *Washington's Writings,* XXXV, 2-5.

[43] Peter Van Schaack to Sedgwick, Kinderhook, N. Y., Apr. 15, 1796, tells of circulation of this speech in handbills and of its great effect. Sedgwich Papers, MHS.

After the necessary funds were appropriated by the House, Washington spoke of the public mind as having been agitated at this time "in a higher degree than it has been at any period since the Revolution."[44] The agitation was stirred up by both parties and there are letters extant from those who were in a position to know, showing how the public excitement was induced. Beckley wrote to DeWitt Clinton in April concerning three Republican congressmen he considered unreliable on the coming vote for appropriations to implement the Treaty:

Elected by small majorities, and doubtful from the present circumstance of your state how the political scale will preponderate at another Election, they perhaps wish to steer that course which will best ensure their reëlection. So often and so fatally, my friend, do personal supersede public considerations. You can best judge of and will I am sure pursue, *the most prudent* means to keep our three friends in the true course—If *they* go right, the British treaty will infallibly be rejected. But remember whatever is done, *must be done quickly.* You possibly know their political connections, and from *whence* they can be best encouraged and supported.[45]

The development of party machinery had gone a long way when party leaders began to put pressure in this fashion on representatives through their constituents. The Republicans were not the only ones who employed these tactics, however. At about the same time, Rufus King wrote to Hamilton of one of the men Beckley mentions:

Van Cortlandt will leave this place on Wednesday. Would it not be well to prepare a reception for him which may return him in favor of the Treaty— His friends may be induced to act upon his mind, which balances, as to decide it.[46]

Hamilton was at the same time writing to King, reporting on the situation in New York and giving instructions for the final effort so to arouse public opinion that the recalcitrant representatives should be forced to grant the appropriation for the Treaty.[47] On April 16 he wrote:

[44] Washington to Pinckney, May 22, 1796, Fitzpatrick, *Washington's Writings,* XXXV, 62.

[45] Beckley to DeWitt Clinton, Philadelphia, Apr., 1796, DeWitt Clinton Papers, CUL.

[46] King to Hamilton, dated Apr. 17 with 1795 added in pencil (should be 1796), Hamilton Papers, XXIV, LC.

[47] Hamilton to King, Apr. 16, 18, and 20, 1796, King Papers, New-York Historical Society (hereafter, NYHS).

Our merchants here are not less alarmed than those of Philadelphia & will do all they can. All the insurance people meet today—The merchants and traders will meet tomorrow or the next day. A petition will be prepared and circulated among the other citizens.

On April 18 he stated the steps which must be taken in Philadelphia. First the President must rebuke the House of Representatives:

. . . then have the merchants meet in the . . . cities & second by their resolutions the measures of the President & Senate and further address their fellow citizens to cooperate with them, petitions afterward to be handed throughout the United States. The Senate to hold fast and consent to no adjournment till the expiration of the term of service of the present house unless provision made. The President to cause a confidential communication to be made to the British stating candidly what has happened, his regrets, his adherence, nevertheless to the treaty, his resolution to persist in the execution as far as depends on the Executive & his hope that the faith of the country will be eventually preserved. But all this must begin with the President. P. S. If the Treaty is not executed the President will be called on in regard to his character & the public good to *keep the post* till another House of Representatives has pronounced.[48]

These are the concrete suggestions, in a time of crisis, of the man who professed to believe in majority rule.

The appropriations for the Treaty were passed because Republican members from New York, New Jersey, and Pennsylvania who had been opposed to the Treaty and who had not intended to vote the money to put it into effect were finally brought to do so. Washington thought that it was passed because of "the torrent of Petitions, and remonstrances which were pouring in from all the Eastern and middle States, and were beginning to come pretty strongly from that of Virginia . . ."[49] but it does not seem to have been the pressure of public opinion, stirred up as we have seen by both sides, which changed the views of these men. The vote of the

---

[48] *Ibid.* In the Jeremy Belknap Papers, the volume labeled 1620-1798, 83 ff., there are a number of letters and petitions which enable us to see how the Boston organization to push the Jay Treaty worked. The Church appears to have been the backbone of this organization, with the ministers urging their parishioners to sign petitions requesting the voting of appropriations for the Treaty. Pamphlets in its behalf appear to have been handed out at some of the rural churches. MHS.

[49] Washington to Pinckney, Philadelphia, May 22, 1796, *Washington's Writings,* XXXV, 62.

doubtful members was changed by two means: by the threat that the Senate would not ratify Pinckney's treaty with Spain which gave us the use of the Mississippi, and by talk of breaking up the Union such as was used at the time the passing of Assumption was delayed. Chauncey Goodrich wrote to Oliver Wolcott, Sr., in April:

. . . 'tis well known that the Senate will, as soon as a vote shall be had on the resolution before us, if unfortunate, tack an amendment providing for the British treaty, to the Spanish treaty bill, and inflexibly adhere for all or none. I am not warranted to assert, but I trust they also will arrest the federal city loan bill, land office, perhaps appropriation for the army, refuse to rise; in short, arrest the whole government, and let the people decide.[50]

The way in which these threats affected Republicans may be seen in the letters of Aaron Kitchell, the center of resistance to the Treaty among the representatives from New Jersey, who wrote to Ebenezer Elmer late in March, ". . . my mind recoils from the issue. I must confess I have heard so many hints lately thrown out Seeming to espouse a wish for Separation of the union that I fear it is more than thought of."[51] A little earlier Kitchell had warned his friend Elmer against resolutions from the New Jersey legislature approving or disapproving the Treaty, lest their state offend some of the larger ones. He had heard, furthermore, that Judge Paterson of the Supreme Court had said that Jersey wished to break off from the Southern states and was ready to do so:

I fear a Separation may take place Sooner than wee would wish. In Such a case whether wee are joined to the Eastern or Southern states we are sure to be the Sufferers. I take it for Granted Mr. Patterson had no authority for what he said and he must have been drunk or a fool to make such a declaration.[52]

It was not Kitchell alone who heard rumors that there would be a separation of the Union if the appropriation were not granted. The British consul in Philadelphia, Phineas Bond, relied on the threat of dissolution ". . . for which the leaders of the democratic party, with all that spirit of Disunion and Discontent, which marks their conduct are not yet ripe,"[53] for the granting of the money. Early in March Sedgwick wrote "If

[50] Chauncey Goodrich to Oliver Wolcott, Sr., Philadelphia, Apr. 23, 1796, Gibbs, *Memoirs*, I, 331.

[51] Aaron Kitchell to Ebenezer Elmer, Philadelphia, Mar. 31, 1796, PHS.

[52] Same to same, Mar. 7, 1796, PHS.

[53] Bond to Grenville, Philadelphia, Mar. 31, 1796, British State Papers (transcripts), LC.

Disorganization [meaning a refusal to vote the appropriation] prevails I see not but that it will then be demonstrated that We cannot live in the same family."[54] A month later he stated that the anxiety in the city of Philadelphia was the greatest he had ever seen. "The conversation of a separation is taking place in almost every company and even I am obliged to moderate the zeal and cool the passions of more cool and temperate men."[55]

There had long been a close connection between Sedgwick and Jonathan Dayton, a representative from New Jersey; and when the House met in December, 1795, Sedgwick had the bulk of the Federalist votes for Speaker, which had been cast unanimously for him in caucus, transferred to Dayton, "whom we carried in triumphantly."[56] During the last of March, Dayton, who had been expected by the Republicans to join them in the Treaty fight, told Sedgwick that he would no longer remain indifferent but would take a decided part for the Treaty. A few days later Sedgwick applied to him for aid on the bill, and Dayton then asked " 'what to do to be saved?' " Sedgwick told him to go to Findley, who was from Western Pennsylvania, and tell him that "he alone could save his country from anarchy & probably civil war." If he found Findley malleable, he was to suggest that the latter make the motion "that provision ought to be made for carrying into effect the several late treaties." Sedgwick then suggested to Dayton an outline of the speech Dayton should make at that time, and Dayton said he would "follow my directions explicitly." Sedgwick prided himself that he did not rely upon the patriotism of these men but the reverse:

Dayton is ambitious, bold, and vindictive. Because Jay has prevented the sequestration of debts he has incurred his mortal enmity. But New Jersey is alarmed and Dayton must regain her confidence or he is finished politically. . . . Findley knows that the Spanish treaty will meet the same fate as the British— the Senate will provide for the whole or none. The Spanish treaty is necessary to Findley's constituents and the opposition of the representative has already created prodigious sensibility. How disgusting it is, my friend, that on the weakness & wickedness of unprincipled men in a popular government the happiness of millions may frequently depend.[57]

[54] Sedgwick to ————, Philadelphia, Mar. 2, 1796, Sedgwick Papers, MHS.
[55] Sedgwick to Ephraim Williams, Philadelphia, Apr. 1, 1796, *ibid.*
[56] Sedgwick to Loring Andrews, Philadelphia, Dec. 7, 1795, *ibid.*
[57] Same to same, Philadelphia, Apr. 5, 1796, *ibid.*

Sedgwick's last letter on these maneuvers stated that the vote had been delayed until Monday because Dayton thought his influence would get the necessary votes by then. "New Jersey is perfectly electrified and Dayton is anxious to retrieve his character as are Kitchell, Samuel Smith and we hope even Findley and Gallatin . . . it seems impossible to live long in the same family with these scoundrels."[58]

If Sedgwick did not exaggerate his part in getting the appropriation for the Jay Treaty passed and did not misrepresent the considerations which caused several Republicans to change their votes, the effect of the famous "tomahawk speech" of Fisher Ames, which is frequently credited with passing the bill, has been greatly overestimated. Ames's tone throughout the speech was one warning of the dire effects which would follow refusal to appropriate the money. Without the treaty, he stated, the Union would be endangered and Indian warfare would be brought to the frontiers. The concern of the frontiersmen for our commercial rights is well known; we see here the invalid recluse of Dedham pleading with frontier representatives for the lives of their wives and children.[59] Gallatin remarked in his answer to this famous speech:

I cannot help considering the cry of war, the threats of a dissolution of government, and the present alarm, as designed for the same purpose, that of making an impression on the fears of this house. It was through the fear of being involved in a war that the negotiation with Great Britain originated; under the impression of fear the treaty has been negotiated and signed; a fear of the same danger, that of war, promoted its ratification; and now every imaginary mischief which can alarm our fears is conjured up, in order to deprive us of that discretion which this House thinks it has a right to exercise, and in order to force us to carry the treaty into effect.[60]

The means by which support for the appropriation was won should be kept in mind when we read such statements as the following:

. . . he [Hamilton] cemented the Federalist group in Congress, and gave it such a pointed efficiency that even when the majority was in fact made up of

---

[58] *Ibid.* Gallatin's constituents were so eager to get the treaty with Spain ratified that they put a great deal of pressure on him to vote for the Jay Treaty. Gallatin Papers, V, March through April, 1796, NYHS.

[59] Ames on Jay Treaty, *Annals of Congress*, Apr. 28, 1796.

[60] Henry Adams, *The Life of Albert Gallatin* (Philadelphia and London, 1880), 165.

Jeffersonians, he was able to dominate it and manoeuver it, as is proved by the long discussions and final votes on the Jay treaty.[61]

The above statement was made to prove the contention that Hamilton was a more able party leader than Jefferson; and if use of influence and coercion be the test of party leadership, he unquestionably was. An American counterpart of the scene so frequent in eighteenth-century London, the mob rioting outside a subservient House of Commons, apparently had no terrors for Hamilton. The question of Jefferson's party leadership at this time can hardly be discussed. As we have seen, it was the Jay Treaty more than anything else which made a party leader of him. In addition to this circumstance we must remember that Hamilton and Jefferson were party leaders of such different types that it is very difficult to compare them profitably, in spite of the common tendency to do so. Hamilton must be admitted to have had an undisputed supremacy in the use of the sort of management and pressure which we have seen exhibited in the struggle over the Treaty, but it ought always to be noted that the technique exhibited here is not, under a representative government, the whole story of party leadership. There is no indication that Hamilton ever realized how expensive this Federalist victory was to prove.

The immediate political results of the Jay Treaty may be seen in the changes of party affiliation which it brought about and in the way in which approval or disapproval of it became an issue in the elections of 1796. It altered party alignments and caused each group to close ranks. Because of the stand of the two parties on the Jay Treaty, such men as John Dickinson, Charles Pinckney, and John Langdon became active Republicans, although each was essentially conservative and each came from a state still dominated by the Federalists. Only one of these men, Pinckney, carried his own state for Jefferson in 1800, but each of them was a source of great strength to the Republicans through the country as a whole from 1796 to 1800.

Probably more important in the eventual Federalist defeat than the open defection of such leaders as these was the Federalist loss at this time

[61] Bernard Faÿ, "Early Party Machinery in the United States," *Pennsylvania Magazine of History and Biography*, LX (Oct., 1936), 377. Faÿ refers to Edgar Eugene Robinson, *The Evolution of American Political Parties* (New York, 1924), 65. Henry Jones Ford writes, "Hamilton's success in carrying his measures through Congress, by sheer dexterity of management when numbers were against him, added bitterness to the natural chagrin felt by the defeated faction." *Washington and His Colleagues, A Chronicle of the Rise and Fall of Federalism* (New Haven, 1918), 165.

of many less prominent men who had nevertheless been the backbone of the party. The disastrous effect of the Jay Treaty upon the Federalist party in the South may be estimated by the statement of Judge Iredell, who wrote, ". . . the sentiments *publicly* expressed by Mr. John Rutledge [who had attacked the Treaty], which procured his rejection by the Senate as Chief Justice, although nominated by General Washington, were shared by almost every other man south of the Potomac, even by those personally friendly to Mr. Jay and stanch Federalists."[62]

One of the immediate effects of the Treaty upon party organization was that it occasioned the first of the two Republican caucuses of the decade, thus taking the development of party machinery a step further.[63] In the Republican campaign to elect members of the House in 1796, attacks upon those who had voted for the Treaty were more prominent than any other form of appeal. In Pennsylvania, Republicans were rallied with the call to throw out "Gregg the Trimmer," and to substitute for Frederick Muhlenberg, Blair McClenachan, who had recommended "kicking the treaty to hell." The Republicans relied on this type of appeal almost as much in New York, where they were unsuccessful, as in Pennsylvania, which they carried.

It was not only the Republicans who made an issue of the Treaty in the election of 1796. Hugh Williamson wrote in October, 1796, "Yesterday I returned from the Eastern States, having been about 200 miles beyond Boston. Nothing was talked of six weeks ago, but the measures of placing federal Members in the Place of those who voted against supporting the Treaty."[64] A little later William Vans Murray wrote from the Eastern Shore of Maryland that he "never knew an election so much of *principles*," that although the Federalists had a candidate who was very unpopular personally, ". . . yet the language is, our choice is a party question, not a personal matter. . . ."[65] William Bentley, the Unitarian minister of Salem, Massachusetts, noted that a new element appeared to have entered politics. "Electioneering goes on in our own state & in New Hamp-

---

[62] Quoted in Mrs. St. Julien Ravenel, *The Life and Times of William Lowndes of South Carolina, 1782-1822* (Boston and New York, 1901), 33-34.

[63] Henry Adams, ed., *The Writings of Albert Gallatin,* 3 vols. (Philadelphia, 1879), III, 553. The other was held when news of the XYZ dispatches reached this country.

[64] Bernard Christian Steiner, *The Life and Correspondence of James McHenry* (Cleveland, 1907), 200.

[65] Nov. 2, 1796, *ibid.,* 200-01.

shire. It extends itself in Boston for the petty officers of the Town. This is the commencement of a new career."[66] Jefferson wrote later of the period following the struggle over the Jay Treaty:

One source of great change in social intercourse arose . . . tho' its effects were as yet scarcely sensible on society or government. I mean the British treaty, which produced a schism that went on widening and rankling till the years '98, '99, when a final dissolution of all bonds, civil & social, appeared imminent.[67]

If the Jay Treaty was of the importance in shaping the two parties which these quotations would indicate, we should inquire as to what was involved in the choice which this country had to make. What did acceptance or rejection of the Jay Treaty mean? What were the aims of the Republican party in taking its stand on this very important issue? Was the opposition merely making political capital out of the necessities of the Administration? Were they simply making it more difficult to do something which had to be done?

The important question is, of course, whether or not war with Great Britain or a serious disruption of our trade with her were the sole alternatives to the Treaty. The only positive evidence on this point would be the statements of such men as Pitt or Lord Grenville as to what their course toward us would have been if we had not offered to open negotiations for a new treaty in 1794, or if we had refused to accept the treaty which resulted from these negotiations. There is no record that any reliable statement was ever made of what British policy would have been in this contingency; and under the circumstances, all that we can do is to look at the conditions in which that country found itself in 1793-94.

It would appear that Great Britain was more hard pressed abroad, more divided and straitened at home, and more isolated diplomatically in 1795 than she had been in 1775 or was to be in 1812. At the time when the Federalists were threatening that we would have war with Great Britain if we did not accept the Treaty, British leaders were wondering how long they would be able to maintain the war merely against France. In July, 1795, Lord Auckland wrote:

[66] William Bentley, *Diary*, Mar. 12, 1796, VI, 174, quoted in William Alexander Robinson, *Jeffersonian Democracy in New England* (New Haven, 1916), 12.

[67] Jefferson to Benjamin Hawkins, Washington, Feb. 18, 1803, Jefferson, *Writings*, IX, 445.

I will not be answerable that we can much longer find funds, however necessary, for the war on a large scale, without serious ill-humor, the tendency to which is much promoted by the very short produce in Europe and America of the last year's harvests, and by the harshness of the present summer.[68]

Under the circumstances, we may seriously question whether Great Britain would have wished to acquire another enemy. To bring about war with us in 1795 or 1796, she would have had to take the initiative in a way in which she did not have to either in 1775 or in 1812. This war would have been against her heaviest debtor and her best customer at a time when she was on the verge of bankruptcy, against the country which was her one certain source of food at a time when provisions were desperately scarce and very expensive. These were the years in which Great Britain was forced to adopt the Speenhamland system of outdoor relief to prevent general starvation. She had just been disastrously defeated in the French West Indies, one of the prizes for which she had gone to war and for which she had diverted men and supplies which would have been very useful to her on the Continent.[69] Would she have wished us to aid either France or the Negroes who were revolting in Santo Domingo?

According to Mahan in his *Influence of Sea Power upon the French Revolution and Empire*, Great Britain went to war with France in 1793 with less than one-fourth of the seamen she had had in active service during the last year of the American Revolution.[70] The conduct of her navy during the early years of this war, culminating in the mutiny at the Nore in 1797, was anything but reassuring. Would she have wished to spread these naval forces thinner, as she would have had to do to fight us? She would have had to make the decision before her victories of Camperdown, Cape St. Vincent, and the Battle of the Nile.

On the other hand, until Hamilton divulged to Hammond that we would not act with the League of Armed Neutrality, we stood in a

[68] Lord Auckland to Hugh Elliott, Jul. 16, 1795, *Journal and Correspondence of Lord Auckland*, III, 309, quoted in Worthington Chauncey Ford, ed., *The Writings of John Quincy Adams*, 7 vols. (New York, 1913-17), I, 412, *n*.

[69] Sir John William Fortescue gives an estimate of the cost of the West Indian campaigns, ". . . which were the essence of Pitt's military policy," and shows how inadequate was the return for this effort. "For this England's soldiers had been sacrificed, her treasure squandered, her influence in Europe weakened, her arm for six hateful years fettered, numbed, and paralysed." *A History of the British Army*, 13 vols. (London and New York, 1899-1930), IV, Part I, 565.

[70] Alfred Thayer Mahan, *The Influence of Sea Power upon the French Revolution and Empire, 1793-1812* (Boston, 1895), 60.

stronger position with regard to Great Britain than we had done at any time between 1783 and 1812. The battle of Fallen Timbers had strengthened us along the entire Northwestern frontier. Englishmen later claimed that Lord Dorchester had spoken without official sanction when he attempted to incite the Indians against us in February, 1794, and that it would have cost him at least his command if hostilities had resulted from his speech. If we had been forced into war during those years, this country would not have been more divided than it was during the Revolution or the War of 1812. Revulsion against France had not yet become general, and a war against Britain would have been a crusade against the old order under slogans that had not yet become suspect in themselves or dishonored by those who bore them. Americans abroad wrote home that there was no fear of retaliation if we refused to sign a treaty which one of them called "the monster begot by Lord Grenville on Mr. Jay."[71] They seemed to be unanimously of the opinion that Great Britain needed our trade as she never had before,[72] though this evidence probably had little to do with the general Republican belief that war would not follow if we refused the Treaty.

The leading Republicans believed that in the condition in which Great Britain found herself, she would not fight us over the issues existing between the two countries at this time even if we rejected the Treaty. They thought, however, that we had already yielded as much as a self-respecting nation could and that if war came, it would be another fight for independence and would be generally regarded as such. No Republican leaders, as far as the writer can discover, ever offered any solution for the problems of government finance which would have arisen in case we had had to fight at that time. Their attitude on the whole question of finance and commercial relations appears to have been what it was during the Revolution, when our trade with the British was regarded mainly as a weapon which might be used against them. The belief in our national self-sufficiency underlay all American assumptions on this point. The spirit of ardent Republicans at this time can best be realized by recalling the attitude of men during the Revolution toward trade with the British. Early in that

[71] Edward Fisher to Rush, Edinburgh, Aug. 30, 1795, Rush MSS., XLV, 29, Philadelphia Library Company, Ridgeway Branch.

[72] *Ibid.*, and J. Speyer to Clinton, London, Feb. 20, 1795, "Should Congress refuse to confirm it, I think we might do anything with this country—for they dare not go to war with us—& wou'd rather give up any point, than hazard to ruin all their manufactures & the residue of their trade." DeWitt Clinton Papers, CUL.

period a Philadelphia Committee of Correspondence wrote to a Committee in Boston:

By sea they will beat us; by land, they will not attempt us; we must try it out in a way of commerce. First, by suspending all trade with Great Britain. . . . Second, by suspending all trade with the West Indies. . . . Third, by withholding flaxseed from Ireland. . . . These are the means we are coolly deliberating; we have other things in contemplation, as stopping our ports entirely and laying up all shipping.[73]

This had been the spirit of Americans at one time, and the belief of the Republicans was that this spirit was as strong and as general as ever. The Republican leaders may have been guilty of a grave miscalculation here, but they were not playing politics with the Jay Treaty. They did not believe that we had given such hostages to fortune that we could not fight again if we had to.

When we attempt to learn what was involved in the choice which this country had to make at the time and what would have happened had we done other than we did, we run the risk of either writing "hypothetical history" or of being wise after the event. It is the former danger which is greater in the attempt to give the Republican view. One need not, however, try to say what would have happened if we had not made the overtures to Britain in the spring of 1794 which resulted in the sending of Jay, or if we had refused to accept the treaty which resulted from Jay's mission. It is enough to say that the Republican leaders believed that Great Britain would not make war, or that if she did, we should be in a much stronger position than we were in 1775, while hers would be weaker. To present these considerations as dominating the views of Republicans, however, is to represent their attitude as much more calculating than it was. In September, 1795, Jefferson wrote concerning the Jay Treaty that he hoped that the result of our policy toward Great Britain "will establish the eternal truth that acquiescence under insult is not the way to escape war."[74] When the terms of the Treaty became generally known in this country, a great many of our citizens felt that we had been merely enjoying the illusion of independence, that this period of illusion was now at an end, and that we were adopting a course which was certain to result

[73] Quoted from Peter Force, *American Archives*, 4th ser., I, 441-42, by Edward Collins, "Committees of Correspondence of the American Revolution," American Historical Association (hereafter, AHA) *Report for 1901*, I, 271.

[74] Jefferson to Henry Tazewell, Sept. 13, 1795, Jefferson, *Writings*, VIII, 191.

in war with France simply because we would not stand up for our rights against England. Which party was right in its view of the Jay Treaty is not so much our concern as is the fact that the clash of their opposing views gave the most powerful stimulus to party division in this country that it had yet received.

3. THE AFTERMATH OF THE JAY TREATY

The basic conditions underlying both our foreign relations and our domestic politics were changed when we accepted the Jay Treaty. Until then, Great Britain was generally regarded as the enemy, actual or potential, and France as our friend and probable ally. Most Americans had thought up to that time that the future of our own experiment depended largely upon the success of the French struggle against monarchy and the old order, that a republican government in this country could not long survive if the coalition of kings should be supreme in Europe. After our acceptance of the Jay Treaty, however, each of these conditions changed in itself or appeared to us in a different light.

It may appear that in putting this emphasis upon our foreign relations after the Jay Treaty, we are wandering far from the development of parties, but the very reverse is true: events growing out of our foreign relations had a decisive influence in determining the course of the two parties in these years. The open split of the Federalist party was on the issue of the second mission to France in 1799. It was such war measures as the Federal land tax of 1799, the Alien and Sedition acts, and above all, the designs of suppression which were supposed to be behind them that finally roused the people of the country against the Federalist regime and swept it from power. It is impossible to separate foreign and domestic relations in this period, for in an epoch of war and revolution, all problems wear a double aspect.

For the period from May, 1796 to March, 1798, our relations with France are the most important phase of government policy. If the Jay Treaty was designed to bring us peace and to remove us from European entanglements, our conduct toward France at this time should have been conciliatory. She may not have deserved this consideration, but our national interest and the widespread desire in this country for peace, which had been so well utilized by Hamilton in the fight for the Treaty, did deserve it. We did not, however, follow a conciliating course. This was true, in part at least, because war with France was the keystone of High-

Federalist policy during the latter years of the decade. This is demonstrated not only by what High-Federalists wrote, but also by their behavior after Adams dashed their hopes by sending the second mission to France. We are not, however, so much concerned with the more or less hypothetical uses to which they might have put this war as with the part these men had in bringing our foreign relations to the desperate situation of 1798 and 1799.

About six weeks after the House passed the appropriations for the Treaty, Hamilton wrote to Wolcott that he wanted three frigates completed at once, the money to be obtained by secret loans from the merchants. Ostensibly for Algerine service, these cruisers were really designed for use against French privateers which hovered around our coasts to prey on British shipping. Hamilton added, "The second object may circulate in whispers."[75] The capturing of an American ship off our coast a few days before by French privateers was apparently to serve as the excuse for our attack upon them. Wolcott answered Hamilton that the affair of the capture was highly equivocal, that although the ship was registered in the name of an American, it had already been sold to an Englishman and after it had crossed the Atlantic was to be delivered to him. "Although the loading was in the name of Willing and Francis, it was in fact British property." He said further that these circumstances were known to or strongly suspected by the owner of the French privateer, that this capture need not alarm us, and that he could not learn that any other had been made.[76] Hamilton, however, continued to stir up feeling against France and wrote to Washington a few days later that Le Guen, a prominent New York merchant, had told him of French plans to seize supplies we were shipping to Great Britain.[77]

As was noted above, propaganda against the French Revolution became greater in volume and more bitter in tone during 1796 than it had been at any time before. It is very difficult to say to what extent this campaign was designed to stir up feeling against France herself and how much of it came naturally from the circumstances of the Presidential campaign of 1796, which was almost completely dominated by considerations of foreign policy. The Republicans claimed that the Treaty put us completely in the hands of Great Britain, that it was a betrayal of our Revolution;

[75] Hamilton to Wolcott, Jun. 16, 1796, Hamilton Papers, LC.
[76] Wolcott to Hamilton, Philadelphia, Jun. 17, 1796, *ibid.*
[77] Hamilton to Washington, Jun. 23, 1796, *ibid.*

the Federalists claimed that opposition to the Treaty came only from those who were the tools of France. The French minister and his agents exerted themselves conspicuously for the election of Jefferson: apparently they had as little idea of the strength of nationalistic sentiment among Americans at this time as Britain showed so frequently between 1789 and 1812. Under the circumstances, Federalist attacks upon the French Revolution were inevitable, but such attacks did not end with the election. They continued and were so plentiful and bitter that it seems probable that they marked some concerted effort, beyond that necessary to defeat Jefferson in 1796, to arouse feeling against France. Until a careful study is made of this propaganda campaign against France from 1796 on, however, it will be impossible to say how far there was a deliberate effort by some Americans to stir up trouble with her and how far Franco-American relations went from bad to worse merely in response to events that had already taken place.

France's refusal to accept C. C. Pinckney as minister in place of Monroe, who had been sacrificed by the Federalists for doing exactly as they wished—keeping France pacified while the Jay Treaty was pushed through—[78] took place early in 1797, and the first of John Adams's problems when he took office in March of that year was to decide what policy

[78] Pickering, who had previously pried into Monroe's private correspondence to get evidence against him, was finally able to get him recalled in the summer of 1796. Monroe had written to George Logan from Paris, Jun. 24, 1795 giving instructions as to the way in which news that he planned to send from France should be made public. Benjamin Bache and John Beckley were to be associated with Logan in the dissemination of this news. Pickering Papers, XLI, 227, MHS. Since the only news which this country had from France came through Britain, and was usually highly colored to suit the purposes of that country, Monroe thought it neecssary that there be some other means by which we could find out what was going on in France. The letter to Logan was opened by Pickering, who kept and used it against Monroe on more than one occasion thereafter. This letter was sent by Pickering to Edward Carrington to discredit Monroe in Virginia. *Ibid.*, III, 530. He stipulated that the letter be returned and that Carrington not let it be known how it came into his possession. The use which Pickering made of it with Washington at the time Monroe was recalled in disgrace is a matter of more importance, though it is not possible to say how much it influenced Washington's decision. Pickering did not send the letter itself to Washington, or tell how it came into his hands, but he did use it as a basis for the most damaging accusations. See Pickering Papers, VI, 189, 191, 193, *ibid.*, for use made of it in influencing Washington. The first of these letters has been printed in Worthington Chauncey Ford, ed., *The Writing of George Washington*, 14 vols. (New York, 1889-93), XIII, 216 *n*. Monroe's conduct as minister cannot be defended in any absolute sense, but it appears to advantage when compared with the conduct of those who were maneuvering to get him dismissed.

we should pursue toward France. Should we send a mission to attempt to reach a suitable basis for further relations, and risk a rebuff, or should we simply let matters drift, with all the risks that such a course would entail? Though Adams and Hamilton were bitter enemies, and the Cabinet subsequently worked with Hamilton against Adams, the question of whether or not to send an extraordinary mission to France presented at this time the spectacle of Adams and Hamilton in agreement and opposed by the Cabinet.[79]

Of the High-Federalist leaders only Fisher Ames appears to have supported the plan of Hamilton and Adams at this time. Wolcott showed one of his few signs of revolting against Hamilton's domination when he wrote to him at the end of March, 1797, after they had had considerable correspondence on the subject, that he was well enough aware of Hamilton's influence to be sure that his plan would be followed or that nothing would be done.[80] Hamilton tried to answer Wolcott's objections by writing ". . . a suspicion begins to dawn among the friends of the government that the actual administration [ministers] is not averse from war with France. How very important to obviate this."[81]

We get a fuller specimen of Hamilton's arguments for the mission in a memorandum of sixteen closely written pages which he prepared and enclosed in a letter to William L. Smith of South Carolina. He concluded his arguments by saying, "The Plan of the government and the Federal party has been to avoid becoming a party in the present war." He feared that if we should become involved:

. . . the wisdom of the plan pursued will be questioned. The confidence in the government will be shaken. The adverse party will acquire the reputation & the influence of superior foresight. . . . The doubt entertained by many of the justifiableness of the treaty with Great Britain in respect to France may increase with suffering and danger & the management of affairs may be thrown into the hands of the opposite party by the voice of the people & government & the country sacrificed to France. Hence it is all important to avoid war if

[79] See Charles Francis Adams, ed., *The Life and Works of John Adams,* 10 vols. (Boston, 1850-56), IX, 286 (hereafter, Adams, *Works*); Wolcott to Hamilton, Philadelphia, Mar. 31, 1797, Gibbs, *Memoirs,* I, 487; Pickering to Hamilton, Philadelphia, Mar. 26, 1797, Hamilton Papers, LC; and Uriah Tracy to Hamilton, Philadelphia, Mar. 23, 1797, *ibid.*
[80] Wolcott to Hamilton, Philadelphia, Mar. 31, 1797, Gibbs, *Memoirs,* I, 487.
[81] Hamilton to Wolcott, New York, Mar. 30, 1797, *ibid.,* I, 485.

we can—if we cannot to strengthen as much as possible the opinion that it proceeds from the Unreasonableness of France. . . .[82]

If Hamilton hoped to avoid war with France, however, his response to Pickering's letters about the XYZ Affair do not indicate it: "I have this moment received your two favors of the 25th. I am delighted with their contents. . . ."[83] Likewise, when Sedgwick first heard of the XYZ Affair, he wrote, "It will afford a glorious opportunity to destroy faction. Improve it."[84] The passing of a few days confirmed him in this view, and he whetted Henry Van Schaack's appetite for news with the report, "Orders will be given immediately to withdraw these envoys from France & there will be told a tale at which every ear will tingle; and unless I am mistaken will give a most fatal blow to the Jacobins."[85]

In June of 1798, Hamilton was sure that the XYZ Affair had destroyed the opposition. "Many of the leaders of faction will pursue and take ultimately a station in the public estimation like that of the Tories of our Revolution."[86] That he was still thinking of relations with France largely in terms of their effect upon the party struggle in this country is indicated by his comment in the margin of a letter King wrote to him in September, 1798, in which the latter stated "You will have no war." Hamilton wrote, "France will treat, not fight; grant us fair terms and not keep them. Meantime our election will occur & bring her friends into power."[87] The statement would seem to imply a belief that only war with France could insure continued Federalist control in this country.

Several circumstances connected with the sending of the mission suggest that Hamilton expected the venture would result in crisis. He had

[82] Hamilton to William L. Smith, Apr. 10, 1797. Hamilton went on to say, "In addition to these [measures for defense which he is urging] it may be proper by some religious solemnity to impress seriously the minds of the people. . . . A politician will consider this as an important means of influencing opinion and will think it a valuable resource in a contest with France to set the Religious ideas of his countrymen in active competition with the atheistical tenets of their enemies. This is an advantage which we shall be very unskillful if we do not use to the utmost. And the impulse cannot be too early given. I am persuaded a day of humiliation and prayer, besides being very proper would be extremely useful." Enclosure, William L. Smith Papers, LC.
[83] Hamilton to Pickering, Mar. 27, 1798, Hamilton, *Works,* VI, 278. The "two favors" Hamilton mentions are *ibid.,* 272, 273.
[84] Sedgwick to ———, Philadelphia, Mar. 7, 1798, Sedgwick Papers, MHS.
[85] Sedgwick to Henry Van Schaack, Philadelphia, Mar. 17, 1798, *ibid.*
[86] Hamilton to King, Jun. 6, 1798, King Papers, XLI, NYHS.
[87] King to Hamilton, London, Sept. 23, 1798, Hamilton Papers, LC.

strongly urged that either Madison or Jefferson be included in the mission, accompanied by two staunch Federalists who could overrule the Republican member. Yet had such a group been successful, either of these two Republican leaders would in all probability have received the larger share of the credit for making peace with France. On the other hand, if a mission which included any eminent Republican leader had failed, the opposition party would have been silenced ahead of time. Is it likely that under these conditions Hamilton would have wanted Madison or Jefferson included if he thought that the mission had any strong probability of success?

Another fact which makes it appear that he was hoping for the failure rather than the success of the mission was his insistence that C. C. Pinckney be included. Pinckney had been embittered by the refusal of the French to accept him at the time Monroe was ordered home, and he had been loud in his complaints against the French. Sending him back at the head of the new mission was like sending Genêt back to us with additional marks of confidence after we had requested that he be withdrawn. Further, the mission was to ask additional concessions from a country which already felt itself to be the injured party. Our envoys were to ask France to let our ships go unmolested to Great Britain while the British seized our ships bound for the French ports. They were to offer nothing in return for these concessions except protestations of good will which were being constantly belied by the conduct of our government, particularly by that of Pickering, Secretary of State, who used diplomatic correspondence which should have been kept secret to stir up the people of the country further against France.[88] These circumstances do not justify

[88] Murray to J. Q. Adams, Jun. 29, 1798, Worthington Chauncey Ford, ed., "Letters of William Vans Murray to John Quincy Adams, 1797-1803," AHA *Report for 1912*, 425-26. For Pickering's use of diplomatic correspondence as campaign documents, see Henry J. Ford's account of Pickering in Samuel Flagg Bemis, ed., *The American Secretaries of State and Their Diplomacy*, 10 vols. (New York, 1927-29), II, 230-31. Hereafter, Bemis, *American Secretaries of State*. The Federalists, lacking the appeal of Washington's name and facing a financial crisis, were in need of a popular issue to take to the people. The Congress, in 1797, was doing nothing to support the Administration's foreign policy (see Fisher Ames to Hamilton, Philadelphia, Jan. 26, 1797, Hamilton Papers, LC; and Samuel Otis to William Smith, Philadelphia, Jun. 20, 1797, Smith-Carter Collection, MHS). Anything that would injure our relations with France or discredit the revolutionary regime would help to serve the purpose of the Federalists, and in fact, as Arthur P. Whitaker has pointed out, steps leading to hostilities with Spain, France's ally, in Florida were already being undertaken by members of the Cabinet. Arthur P. Whitaker, *The Mississippi Question, 1795-1803* (New York, 1934), 125-27.

Talleyrand's treatment of our envoys, but they do make it seem improbable that there was ever much hope of success for a mission constituted and instructed as was this one.

Hamilton's own temperament and his policies both before and after the mission to France make it appear probable that his sending of the mission was merely a maneuver in a complicated game which embraced both our foreign relations and our domestic politics. He appears to have valued highly a maxim which he copied into one of his notebooks from Demosthenes:

As a general marches at the head of his troups, so ought wise politicians, if I dare use the expression, to march at the head of affairs: insomuch that they ought not to wait the event to know what measures to take: but the measures which they have taken, ought to produce the event.[89]

The sending of a mission that had little chance of success would have been such a shaping of events as Demosthenes here recommends. It would have been in harmony with Hamilton's earlier policies, for he had tried from an early date to ally us with Britain against France.[90] His conduct in giving Beckwith and Hammond information which weakened our diplomatic position from 1792 to 1795 suggests that he thought that being a tail to the British kite was our natural role in foreign relations at this time.

John Adams had also favored the sending of a mission to France, but there is no reason to believe that he conceived all the possibilities that Hamilton did in such a move, or that he urged it in any but complete good faith. He was enraged by the behavior of the French in the XYZ Affair, but he did not push hostilities against France after he saw the possibility of an honorable peace. He never used the war fever as an excuse for entrenching himself politically, and it was he and he alone who put an end to the schemes of Hamilton and his associates in 1799, though he terminated his own political career in doing so. Adams was among those who had accepted the Jay Treaty reluctantly, who regarded it as preferable to war with Britain but did not think of it as furnishing the occasion for war with France or for a complete reorientation of our policies which should put us under British domination. Unless further research into our foreign relations and our anti-French propaganda from 1796 to 1799

[89] An extract from Demosthenes copied in Hamilton's Memorandum Book, 250, LC.

[90] Dexter Perkins, *Hands Off, A History of the Monroe Doctrine* (Boston, 1941), 13-14.

should disclose new evidence, we shall not be able to say what use Hamilton meant to make of the Jay Treaty. In the meantime, however, there seems to be ample ground to question whether he wished us to pursue the policy of neutrality and isolation which he had recommended in Washington's Farewell Address and whether he meant to further such a policy by his support of either the Jay Treaty or the first mission to France.

Our relations with England did not form a separate problem from our relations with France during those years. Our relations with each country were rather two aspects of a single fundamental problem, that of our neutrality or our participation in the European war; and this was in a sense the problem also of whether we were to be truly independent or were to be dominated by Great Britain. It was hard enough for us to stand on our own feet as a neutral, but once in the maelstrom of the European wars of this period, we should have been utterly unable to do so.

As our relations with France became more tense in 1797 and 1798, those with Britain became easier in their superficial aspect. They eased only superficially, however, for British offers and concessions, such as they were, were all made on the supposition that we were about to join them in a war upon France. For our rights as a neutral nation, as we conceived them, the British were to show the contempt which appears to have been their official attitude until after the War of 1812. Aside from finally giving us the western posts which we had been promised in 1783, the Jay Treaty did nothing to remove our basic difficulties with Great Britain. Some of the problems it was supposed to settle, such as our debts to Britain, were further complicated and confused by the commissions set up under the Treaty to handle them.

John Quincy Adams in London and Noah Webster in New York each wrote a description of British commercial policy as it touched our interest at this time. Adams warned that the concessions which England now had to make regarding our West Indian trade would be cut off the moment the British could obtain control of the French Islands:

One of the favorite objects of this government is an increase of their dominions in the East and West Indies. . . . There is no such thing as commercial liberality in the country. To engross the commerce of the world to themselves is the professed or secret wish of every heart among them.[91]

[91] J. Q. Adams to Pickering, London, Dec. 22, 1795, Pickering Papers, XX, 118-19, MHS.

A few years later Noah Webster wrote to Rufus King, then ambassador to Great Britain, deploring the shortsighted policy behind British depredations and restrictions on our commerce. He said that all we needed from Great Britain was that she give our vessels the freedom and privileges of "what is called the modern law of nations. . . . The jealousies and restrictions of Great Britain always appeared to me like the policy of a countertrader, who should attempt to limit the industry or destroy the Harvest of his customers."[92]

Republican denunciations of Great Britain's commercial policy are apt to be too heated and partisan, and the remarks of such moderate Federalists as Adams and Webster, who, though they were anti-French, were not blind to the dangers and difficulties of close Anglo-American relations, are perhaps as good contemporary evidence as can be found on this point.

In the face of these fundamental aspects of British policy, it may seem strange to us that the High-Federalists, many of them men with shipping and financial interests, should have been so pro-British in their views, though their attitude may have been due in part to their hope of greater concessions from Great Britain, which were at this time dangled before them. In April, 1797, Liston wrote to Grenville:

. . . the men of fortune, of weight and character now begin so generally to come forward to a close connection with Great Britain as the only wise system of American politicks, that I have considered it as necessary to the King's service, and consistent with the spirit of the instructions I have received from your lordship, that I should recommend it to the Commanders of His Majesty's ships upon this station to afford to the merchant vessels of the United States, especially to those bound for our West India Islands all the protection that is consistent with the general orders they may have received from home.[93]

Other concessions followed or were promised. A few days later Rufus King, our ambassador in London, was entering in his journal the information that Lord Dorchester's taking the forts at Miami was contrary to orders he had seen at the Duke of Portland's office. He said that General Simcoe told him that if war with the United States had followed, Lord Dorchester would have forfeited his head,[94] a remark which at least indi-

[92] Webster to King, Jun. 1797, King Papers, XLI, 22, NYHS.

[93] Liston to Grenville, Philadelphia, Apr. 18, 1797, British State Papers (transcripts), LC.

[94] A long entry on unnumbered pages, Rufus King's Journal, May 3, 1797, King Papers, LXXIII, NYHS.

cates British policy in 1797. In June of that year King was notified by
George Rose, a British official, that "Vessels coming from the States of
America will not now be subject to a higher duty than those from Ham-
burgh or the nearest ports of Europe." This was presented as a great
concession. He further stated "I cannot bring myself to think that the
measures as at first proposed [against which King had protested vigor-
ously] trenched in the slightest degrees either on the letter or spirit of the
Treaty rightly understood." Rose went on to say that other duties originally contemplated in the bill had been given up, and that he would rejoice
if these considerable sacrifices of Britain promoted friendly relations. "We
may, and I hope we shall, be a Tower of strength to each other."[95]

In June, 1798, Grenville wrote to Liston suggesting that, since war
seemed certain between the United States and France, British ships be
used as convoys for American vessels and, in return, American seamen be
used to man other British vessels. Grenville thought that France would
not declare war on the United States, but that the United States would
find it to her own interest to declare war on France. He said that Great
Britain and France might make peace, but that if the United States should
enter into any engagements with Great Britain, they would be scrupu-
lously observed by the latter. "You may with the fullest confidence assure
the president that any proposals for concert and cooperation will be cor-
dially received here."[96] A letter from Grenville in October stated that the
British would loan the Americans cannon which they had at Halifax, but
that these might be recalled at any time the King desired them.[97] Later another letter from Grenville urged Liston to disclaim any intention of
Great Britain to bind the United States in any permanent system of
alliance.[98]

Perhaps the most tempting bait Britain had to offer, although it was
couched in the vaguest terms, was the hint that we might be admitted to a
share in some of their more lucrative commercial monopolies. Pickering
wrote to Washington, "It will give you additional pleasure to learn that
such is the increased and increasing respectability of the United States
among the European powers that from being viewed with indifference
and even contempt, our friendship and commerce are courted." And later
in the same letter he says:

[95] George Rose to Rufus King, Jun. 22, 1797, Box VII, 83, *ibid.*
[96] Grenville to Liston, Jun. 8, 1798, British State Papers (transcripts), LC.
[97] Same to same, Oct. 20, 1798, *ibid.*
[98] Same to same, Dec. 8, 1798, *ibid.*

Another striking proof of our national importance I must not omit; Mr. Pitt has made to Mr. King a proposition which implies an opinion that in certain articles (sugar & coffee in particular) Great Britain & the States may regulate the commerce of Europe. The subject has not been fully investigated—facts were sought for. But the idea presented by Mr. Pitt, whether it shall ever become a [illegible] or not demonstrates our commercial and even our political importance.[99]

To the High-Federalists it seemed that we were being admitted into partnership with Britain, albeit as a junior partner. The fact that our whole position and prosperity as they envisaged it would be entirely dependent upon Britain appears not to have bothered them in the slightest degree. Compared with John Adams, these men were colonials.

At the time that Great Britain was making or promising such concessions as these, the price that we were expected to pay for them and the consequences if we did not pay it were also being made clear to all who were inclined to see them. Britain was at this time relying heavily upon the prospect of our naval aid. Our forces had already joined with hers in operations against the French privateers in the West Indies; the two navies had drawn up a set of signals by which they would recognize each other,[100] and the British wished us to furnish the seamen to arm ten or twelve of their ships,[101] these to remain under the command of their officers. The solution for our two most crying grievances, captures and impressment, was thus clearly indicated. We had only to furnish first-class seamen for their shorthanded navy and to send our vessels in their convoys, by which our cargoes would of course be taken to British ports where they would be used or re-exported as the British wished.

If we followed those policies there would be no conflicts with the British. They did not, of course, put the alternative to us so directly. They merely made the offers and continued to capture and impress when we did not take advantage of them. British captures and impressments grew much worse after Adams showed his willingness to treat with France, but they had not ceased even before then. In November of that year, a

[99] Pickering to Washington, Philadelphia, Feb. 8, 1799, Pickering Papers, X, 365-67, MHS.
[100] Cited from Dudley Wright Knox, *Naval Documents* (Washington, 1935-38), I, 336 by Rayford Whittington Logan, *The Diplomatic Relations of the United States with Haiti, 1776-1891* (Chapel Hill, 1941), 92.
[101] Grenville to Liston, Jun. 8, 1798, British State Papers (transcripts), LC.

British squadron took a part of the crew from the American man-of-war *Baltimore*. "President Adams thereupon ordered all American commanders 'to resist every future attempt of the kind to the last extremity.'"[102]

Thus we were being offered a snug place within the imperial framework on the one hand, while being warned on the other, by British practices, of the difficulties and dangers of an independent policy.

In addition to offers of the protection of the British navy and vague hints of a future commercial partnership, Britain was inviting us to share in a vast and daring enterprise in Latin America. Miranda, the Spanish-American revolutionary leader, had been trying for some years to get British support for his scheme to overthrow Spanish rule in South America. In 1797, after France and Spain became allies, Pitt showed a renewed interest in this project. By the summer of 1798, Rufus King was writing frequent letters, particularly to Pickering and Hamilton, urging that we join in the venture against Spanish possessions. It is not surprising, in view of the interest of certain of our Cabinet members in Louisiana and Florida, that the plan of Miranda and Pitt was welcomed most enthusiastically by some Americans. King wrote of it late in 1798, "As *England is ready she will* furnish *a fleet and military stores and we should* furnish *the army.*"[103] And in January, 1799, he wrote to Hamilton:

For God's sake, attend to the very interesting subject treated of in my ciphered dispatches to the Secretary of State of the 10th, 18th, and 19th instant. Connect it, as it should be, with the main object, the time to accomplish which has arrived. Without superstition, Providence seems to have prepared the way, and to have pointed out the instruments of its will. Our children will reproach us if we neglect our duty, and humanity will escape many scourges if we act with wisdom and decision. I am more confirmed than before, that an efficient force will be confederated to act against France. The combination is *not yet completed,* but, as I have reason to believe, will soon be.

That will be the moment for us to settle upon immutable foundations the extensive system of the American nation. Who can hinder us? One nation alone has the power; and she will coöperate in the accomplishment in South America of what has so well been done in North.[104]

---

[102] Quoted from Liston Papers, Jan.-Jun., 1799, LC., by Arthur Burr Darling, *Our Rising Empire, 1763-1803* (New Haven and London, 1940), 304.

[103] King to Pickering, London, Oct. 20, 1798, King, *Correspondence*, II, 453-54.

[104] King to Hamilton, London, Jan. 21, 1799, *ibid.*, 519.

Thus King, with Pickering, Ames, and many others, thought that our true destiny lay in close union with Great Britain. The destruction of France and the commercial exploitation with Great Britain of the French and Spanish colonies in this hemisphere seemed to him a dazzling opportunity.

There was at the same time still another plan afoot for Anglo-American collaboration, this time in support of Toussaint against the French in Santo Domingo.[105] It is impossible to say what actually went on there, or what the precise plans of the High-Federalists were regarding it; but our activities, whether rightly understood or not, had important consequences in our politics in this country. The South regarded any sort of encouragement to Toussaint as an invitation to their own slaves to revolt. Many of the Virginians thought that the New England Federalists would be glad to see slave insurrections in the South, and in their minds Adams bore the blame for much that went on in Santo Domingo of which he had no knowledge. Here as elsewhere, he bore the brunt of the responsibility both for what the High-Federalists were actually doing and for the plans attributed to them.

On the other hand, the designs which Adams himself attributed to the High-Federalists in connection with Santo Domingo appear to have had a prominent place among the considerations which caused him to send a

---

[105] General Maitland came to this country to arrange for our joint support of Toussaint. In June, 1798, Congress passed an act suspending commercial intercourse between the United States and France, and in the next session an act was passed continuing it but making it possible for the President to except from it any former French possession which became independent. (Pickering to Edward Stevens, Philadelphia, Mar. 7, 1799, Pickering Papers, X, 461-64, MHS.)

Most of the steps which we took in this affair appear to have been carried out behind Adams's back. It is very doubtful, for instance, that he ever knew that Hamilton had been asked by Pickering to draw up a scheme of government for Santo Domingo, or that he had intended, in opening trade with that island, to put Toussaint in the power of our merchants and politicians. (Pickering to Hamilton, Feb. 9, 1799, ibid., 368.)

All our dealings regarding Santo Domingo were in the hands of Pickering, who apparently took his orders from Hamilton. Hamilton kept all the strings in his own hands in this delicate commercial and diplomatic venture by having Edward Stevens, a boyhood friend and, like himself, a native of the West Indies, appointed a representative of the State Department in Santo Domingo. Our relations with Santo Domingo were to wear a somewhat different guise officially from what they were among the inner circle who were controlling them, for Hamilton instructed Pickering that the United States "must not be committed on the Independence of St. Domingo—no guarantee, no formal treaty—nothing that can rise up in judgment." (Hamilton to Pickering, Feb. 9, 1799, ibid., XXIV, 65.)

mission to France in 1799. Something that he wrote years later would indicate that the plans in operation in Santo Domingo had influenced his decision upon crucial points in his conduct as President:

As I had been intimately connected with Mr. Jefferson in friendship and affection for five-and-twenty years, I well knew his crude and visionary notions of government as well as his learning, taste, and talent in other arts and sciences. I expected his reign would be very nearly what it has been. I regretted it, but could not help it. At the same time, I thought it would be better than following the fools who were intriguing to plunge us into an alliance with England, an endless war with all the rest of the world, and wild expeditions to South America and St. Domingo; and, what was worse than all the rest, a civil war, which I knew would be the consequence of the measures the heads of that party wished to pursue.[106]

Whatever the causes for Adams's decision, the sending of the second mission to France put an end to British efforts at collaboration with this country. Their captures of our ships and impressment of our seamen became again as numerous as at any time during the decade. The heavy captures of the British in 1800 were an important factor in bringing about the Republican victory in the election, particularly since one of these captures influenced the vote of New York City, upon which depended that of the state and less directly that of the whole country.

These seizures were by no means the only ground for contention between the two countries. Other causes of trouble and ill will against Great Britain arose out of the Jay Treaty. In regard to the question of the return to this country of Tories banished during the Revolution, as in some matters of commerce, the British were putting a construction on the Treaty which even such defenders of it as Jay and Hamilton did not think it could reasonably be made to bear. The sixth article, which provided for the collection of debts owed before the Revolution, was particularly troublesome, and negotiations on this point finally broke down completely.

Republicans, particularly the more partisan and unscrupulous ones, made the fullest use of the difference between the two countries which arose from different constructions of the various articles of the Jay Treaty. Several circumstances lent themselves to the charge that all the different ways in which the British injured or irritated us were a matter of design. *The Anti-Jacobin Review,* a British periodical which had some circulation

[106] Adams to James Lloyd, Quincy, Mar. 31, 1815. Adams, *Works,* X, 154-55.

here, contained much abuse and ridicule of this country and its prominent figures, and it did not confine itself to Republicans. As the journal
was something of an official organ during the most reactionary phase of
the Pitt administration, some Americans claimed that the British ministry
at least approved of this abuse.[107] Some of the articles on America favored
a close relationship with Britain.

The policy of the Pitt administration toward neutral countries added
to the apprehension of the well-informed in this country, as the Prime
Minister had declared it "a principle that the distance between friends and
neutrals is immense; it is small, on the contrary, between enemies and
neutrals; the slightest accident, a mere chance, the least mistrust, a false
appearance, is enough to efface the distinction between them."[108] A High-
Federalist of Philadelphia, Thomas Fitzsimmons, expressed the bewilder-
ment at British policies which was felt by those in this country who had
tried hardest to defend them.

To me it appears strange that the British ministry have never thought it their
interest to try and conciliate this country; they cannot be uninformed of the
state of parties here, or insensible to the advantages they derive from a good
understanding with us. A very considerable portion of the commerce of this
country is carried on with their manufacturers, and the payment for these
insures them no small proportions of our exports. With all this their conduct
is invariably cold and suspicious. They even never miss an opportunity of cir-
cumscribing our happiness, and though they may not directly sanction the
depredations of their cruizers, they certainly take no pains to prevent them.
I am not without my apprehensions too, that their necessity as well as their
monopolizing spirit will, when there is a peace, draw a circle round our commerce, that for a time at least, will narrow it down to a very small compass.
. . . If the British restrict our trade, let us meet them with restrictions on our
part, and if we cannot find employment for our capital in commerce, let us
employ it in either agriculture or manufactures.[109]

This conclusion was one which had been shared by many in the years
preceding the Constitution and had been consistently urged by Jefferson
and Madison from 1789 to 1800. Republicans would have said that we had

---

[107] King to Pickering, London, Oct. 11, 1799, King, *Correspondence*, III, 124.

[108] Quoted from *Godoy's Memoirs*, I, 468, by Andrew Jackson Montague in his
article on John Marshall in Bemis, *American Secretaries of State*, II, 359.

[109] Thomas Fitzsimmons to Wolcott, Philadelphia, Jul. 24, 1800, Gibbs, *Memoirs*,
II, 389.

passed by our best opportunities to win concessions from the British in the period from 1790 to 1795 and would have put the blame largely upon Hamilton. Most modern historians would deny such a statement, however, and would hold that, given Great Britain's commercial and naval power and the policies which naturally accompanied them, our relations with her were bound to have been about what they were from 1789 to 1800, regardless of the policies we sought to pursue.

Although our relations with France and England were not much different in 1800 from what they had been in 1795, the vicissitudes of those years had had a far-reaching effect in this country. The XYZ Affair had weaned all but the most deluded Republicans from an excessive attachment to France, and Britain's conduct had convinced even High-Federalists, at least for the moment, that we must stand on our own feet and not attempt to lean on Britain. At the first view it would appear that foreign relations had been the point upon which our domestic politics had turned between 1795 and 1800; for the Jay Treaty, the XYZ Affair, and the sending of the second mission to France had each in turn dominated and reshaped domestic politics for a time. Yet the first and last and perhaps the second of these three events were rooted as deeply in the domestic as in the international situation, and by 1800 the tendency toward nationalism and self-sufficiency was stronger than at any other time since 1789.

We achieve this view if we treat the period from 1789 to 1801 as a unit and if we attempt to trace the connection between our foreign relations and our domestic politics during that time. It is the development of parties and the growth of the party conflict which give continuity to the period and which provide the connection between the realms of foreign and domestic affairs. The party conflict is, of course, evident in the very circumstances of domestic affairs, but its relation to foreign policies has been somewhat obscured by the fact that they, being in the hands of the President and the Cabinet, did not exhibit the same open clash of views as could be seen in debates in the House of Representatives. Further, much of what happened in foreign affairs was kept from the public at the time, so that its influence in the forming of public opinion was not comparable to its intrinsic importance. Yet we should not forget that the High-Federalist leaders viewed their adversaries as enemies of society in league with fellow Jacobins in France, who must be discredited by any means. One of the most attractive features of a war with France to such men as Hamilton, Sedgwick, Ames, and Cabot was the opportunity it offered for "cleaning house" and putting it beyond the power of "demagogues and disorganizers" ever to seize control of the government. Many Federalists regarded their control of foreign affairs as their surest weapon against the Republicans. We cannot, however, go so far as to say that war with France was to be merely a blind, an excuse of the High-Federalists for proceeding against their opponents at home. Rather, they regarded the principles of liberty and equality as infections which must be stamped out wherever they were to be found.

This feeling was evident as early as the time of the Constitutional Convention, but it grew stronger during the decade. During that period the more obvious aspects of the party conflict shifted first from domestic questions to foreign relations and then back to domestic again. Until 1793 our foreign relations did not provide issues so pressing as those which grew out of Hamilton's domestic policy. From 1793 on, the questions of our neutrality, the Jay Treaty, and our relations with France engrossed the larger share of attention until we were faced with the question of war with France in 1798. Momentous as that issue was, public attention was gradually diverted from it by the emergency powers which the Federalists asked and by the means which they took to suppress opposition to their measures. The Federal land tax of 1798, the Alien and Sedition laws, the Ross election bill of 1800, all these and other measures gave the Republicans such an opportunity to arouse the ordinary voter of this country as they had never previously had. Even before news of the XYZ Affair had reached this country the Republicans had seen that they must shift their ground and leave the question of foreign relations, which was for the time taken completely out of the hands of the opposition party. Gallatin had written to his wife from Congress late in 1798, ". . . we mean, if possible, to avoid fighting on foreign ground. Their clamor about foreign influence is the only thing we have to fear, and on domestic affairs exclusively we must resist them."[110]

After the XYZ Affair it was more necessary than ever that the Republicans concentrate upon domestic issues. Feeling against France, whose conduct in the XYZ Affair could not be defended, rose high even among the Republicans themselves, and on the other hand, Federalist domestic policies became more and more open to attack. The reaction of the American people to the war measures of 1798-99, their evident distaste for militarism, their reluctance to pay the Land Tax, and their resentment of the

[110] Dec. 14, 1798, Adams, *Life of Gallatin*, 224.

Alien and Sedition laws do not fall, properly speaking, within the sphere of party origins. The public feeling these measures aroused is closely related to this topic, but its true significance is to be found rather in the fact that it constituted the background for the election of 1800, which was a part of the second rather than the first phase of party development.

If we observe the struggle of the two parties in the effort to shape our foreign policy, we see that the contest is not between abstract forces but between two groups of men. These men professed principles of constitutional interpretation, and they were moved in part by their economic interests, or their conception of them; but neither of these factors gives a full explanation of their conduct. If we regard this as a conflict of abstractions, we run into various pitfalls, not the least of which is that we are likely to interpret the struggle by what the actors in it said, both about themselves and their opponents, rather than by what they did.

We draw nearer the truth of the matter if, instead of viewing this as a contest of abstractions, we regard it as one between two shifting groups of men who, differing upon practical problems as they arose, came to suspect the views and purposes of those in the opposite camp and to regard their own pursuit of power and their determination to defeat their opponents as the supreme consideration. A party becomes an entity like a nation, and, as with a nation, the question of its own survival is likely to be paramount. This is not to say, however, that all the men of this time put the success of their party above every other consideration, but they tended to do so as the party struggle became more and more bitter. If we recognize this fact, we leave room for the play of motives, otherwise disregarded, which were frequently of the greatest importance.

If we put the emphasis upon a conflict of parties, a good deal which would otherwise furnish material for controversy, such as the inconsistencies of both Hamilton and Jefferson, is explained. If we ask what Hamilton was trying to accomplish at a given time—whether he was trying to get the Constitution ratified, or, that done, to "prop up the frail and worthless fabric," as he himself described his later policies—we shall understand his conflicting statements better than if we try to explain them solely in the light of his theories of government or by his concern for any economic interest. We shall also find an answer to the question why Jefferson was more concerned about strict construction while he was in the opposition than he was while he was President. If we place our emphasis upon party conflict, we shall understand how it was that Adams and

Jefferson, both much closer in their economic interests and in their views on government than is generally recognized, were the rival candidates in one of the bitterest and most momentous elections which this country has ever seen. A comparison of their different views as they discussed them in letters to each other with those same differences as they were misrepresented and exaggerated by the partisans of 1800 is one of the best possible illustrations of how party feeling can put men into positions which they would never have taken from choice.

INDEX

INDEX

Revised February 1966

harper ✦ torchbooks

HUMANITIES AND SOCIAL SCIENCES

American Studies: General

THOMAS C. COCHRAN: The Inner Revolution: *Essays on the Social Sciences in History* TB/1140

EDWARD S. CORWIN: American Constitutional History. *Essays edited by Alpheus T. Mason and Gerald Garvey* TB/1136

CARL N. DEGLER, Ed.: Pivotal Interpretations of American History TB/1240, TB/1241

A. HUNTER DUPREE: Science in the Federal Government: *A History of Policies and Activities to 1940* TB/573

OSCAR HANDLIN, Ed.: This Was America: *As Recorded by European Travelers in the Eighteenth, Nineteenth and Twentieth Centuries. Illus.* TB/1119

MARCUS LEE HANSEN: The Atlantic Migration: 1607-1860. *Edited by Arthur M. Schlesinger. Introduction by Oscar Handlin* TB/1052

MARCUS LEE HANSEN: The Immigrant in American History. *Edited with a Foreword by Arthur M. Schlesinger* TB/1120

JOHN HIGHAM, Ed.: The Reconstruction of American History TB/1068

ROBERT H. JACKSON: The Supreme Court in the American System of Government TB/1106

JOHN F. KENNEDY: A Nation of Immigrants. *Illus. Revised and Enlarged. Introduction by Robert F. Kennedy* TB/1118

RALPH BARTON PERRY: Puritanism and Democracy TB/1138

ARNOLD ROSE: The Negro in America: *The Condensed Version of Gunnar Myrdal's An American Dilemma* TB/3048

MAURICE R. STEIN: The Eclipse of Community: *An Interpretation of American Studies* TB/1128

W. LLOYD WARNER and Associates: Democracy in Jonesville: *A Study in Quality and Inequality* ‖ TB/1129

W. LLOYD WARNER: Social Class in America: *The Evaluation of Status* TB/1013

American Studies: Colonial

BERNARD BAILYN, Ed.: The Apologia of Robert Keayne: *Self-Portrait of a Puritan Merchant* TB/1201

BERNARD BAILYN: The New England Merchants in the Seventeenth Century TB/1149

JOSEPH CHARLES: The Origins of the American Party System TB/1049

LAWRENCE HENRY GIPSON: The Coming of the Revolution: 1763-1775. † *Illus.* TB/3007

LEONARD W. LEVY: Freedom of Speech and Press in Early American History: *Legacy of Suppression* TB/1109

PERRY MILLER: Errand Into the Wilderness TB/1139

PERRY MILLER & T. H. JOHNSON, Eds.: The Puritans: *A Sourcebook of Their Writings*
Vol. I TB/1093; Vol. II TB/1094

EDMUND S. MORGAN, Ed.: The Diary of Michael Wigglesworth, 1653-1657: *The Conscience of a Puritan*

EDMUND S. MORGAN: The Puritan Family: *Religion and Domestic Relations in Seventeenth-Century New England* TB/1227

RICHARD B. MORRIS: Government and Labor in Early America TB/1244

KENNETH B. MURDOCK: Literature and Theology in Colonial New England TB/99

WALLACE NOTESTEIN: The English People on the Eve of Colonization: 1603-1630. † *Illus.* TB/3006

LOUIS B. WRIGHT: The Cultural Life of the American Colonies: 1607-1763. † *Illus.* TB/3005

American Studies: From the Revolution to 1860

JOHN R. ALDEN: The American Revolution: 1775-1783. † *Illus.* TB/3011

MAX BELOFF, Ed.: The Debate on the American Revolution, 1761-1783: *A Sourcebook* TB/1225

RAY A. BILLINGTON: The Far Western Frontier: 1830-1860. † *Illus.* TB/3012

EDMUND BURKE: On the American Revolution: *Selected Speeches and Letters.* ‡ *Edited by Elliott Robert Barkan* TB/3068

WHITNEY R. CROSS: The Burned-Over District: *The Social and Intellectual History of Enthusiastic Religion in Western New York, 1800-1850* TB/1242

GEORGE DANGERFIELD: The Awakening of American Nationalism: 1815-1828. † *Illus.* TB/3061

CLEMENT EATON: The Freedom-of-Thought Struggle in the Old South. *Revised and Enlarged. Illus.* TB/1150

CLEMENT EATON: The Growth of Southern Civilization: 1790-1860. † *Illus.* TB/3040

LOUIS FILLER: The Crusade Against Slavery: 1830-1860. † *Illus.* TB/3029

DIXON RYAN FOX: The Decline of Aristocracy in the Politics of New York: 1801-1840. ‡ *Edited by Robert V. Remini* TB/3064

FELIX GILBERT: The Beginnings of American Foreign Policy: *To the Farewell Address* TB/1200

FRANCIS J. GRUND: Aristocracy in America: *Social Class in the Formative Years of the New Nation* TB/1001

ALEXANDER HAMILTON: The Reports of Alexander Hamilton. ‡ *Edited by Jacob E. Cooke* TB/3060

THOMAS JEFFERSON: Notes on the State of Virginia. ‡ *Edited by Thomas P. Abernethy* TB/3052

JAMES MADISON: The Forging of American Federalism: *Selected Writings of James Madison. Edited by Saul K. Padover* TB/1226

---

† The New American Nation Series, edited by Henry Steele Commager and Richard B. Morris.

‡ American Perspectives series, edited by Bernard Wishy and William E. Leuchtenburg.

* The Rise of Modern Europe series, edited by William L. Langer.

‖ Researches in the Social, Cultural, and Behavioral Sciences, edited by Benjamin Nelson.

§ The Library of Religion and Culture, edited by Benjamin Nelson.

Σ Harper Modern Science Series, edited by James R. Newman.

° Not for sale in Canada.

Business, Economics & Economic History

REINHARD BENDIX: Work and Authority in Industry: *Ideologies of Management in the Course of Industrialization* TB/3035

GILBERT BURCK & EDITORS OF FORTUNE: The Computer Age: *And Its Potential for Management* TB/1179

THOMAS C. COCHRAN: The American Business System: *A Historical Perspective, 1900-1955* TB/1080

THOMAS C. COCHRAN: The Inner Revolution: *Essays on the Social Sciences in History* TB/1140

THOMAS C. COCHRAN & WILLIAM MILLER: The Age of Enterprise: *A Social History of Industrial America* TB/1054

ROBERT DAHL & CHARLES E. LINDBLOM: Politics, Economics, and Welfare: *Planning & Politico-Economic Systems Resolved into Basic Social Processes* TB/3037

PETER F. DRUCKER: The New Society: *The Anatomy of Industrial Order* TB/1082

EDITORS OF FORTUNE: America in the Sixties: *The Economy and the Society* TB/1015

ROBERT L. HEILBRONER: The Great Ascent: *The Struggle for Economic Development in Our Time* TB/3030

FRANK H. KNIGHT: The Economic Organization TB/1214

FRANK H. KNIGHT: Risk, Uncertainty and Profit TB/1215

ABBA P. LERNER: Everybody's Business: *Current Assumptions in Economics and Public Policy* TB/3051

ROBERT GREEN MC CLOSKEY: American Conservatism in the Age of Enterprise, 1865-1910 TB/1137

PAUL MANTOUX: The Industrial Revolution in the Eighteenth Century: *The Beginnings of the Modern Factory System in England* [o] TB/1079

WILLIAM MILLER, Ed.: Men in Business: *Essays on the Historical Role of the Entrepreneur* TB/1081

RICHARD B. MORRIS: Government and Labor in Early America TB/1244

HERBERT SIMON: The Shape of Automation: *For Men and Management* TB/1245

PERRIN STRYKER: The Character of the Executive: *Eleven Studies in Managerial Qualities* TB/1041

PIERRE URI: Partnership for Progress: *A Program for Transatlantic Action* TB/3036

Contemporary Culture

JACQUES BARZUN: The House of Intellect TB/1051

JOHN U. NEF: Cultural Foundations of Industrial Civilization TB/1024

NATHAN M. PUSEY: The Age of the Scholar: *Observations on Education in a Troubled Decade* TB/1157

PAUL VALÉRY: The Outlook for Intelligence TB/2016

Historiography & Philosophy of History

JACOB BURCKHARDT: On History and Historians. *Intro. by H. R. Trevor-Roper* TB/1216

WILHELM DILTHEY: Pattern and Meaning in History: *Thoughts on History and Society.* [o] *Edited with an Introduction by H. P. Rickman* TB/1075

J. H. HEXTER: Reappraisals in History: *New Views on History & Society in Early Modern Europe* TB/1100

H. STUART HUGHES: History as Art and as Science: *Twin Vistas on the Past* TB/1207

RAYMOND KLIBANSKY & H. J. PATON, Eds.: Philosophy and History: *The Ernst Cassirer Festschrift. Illus.* TB/1115

GEORGE H. NADEL, Ed.: Studies in the Philosophy of History: *Selected Essays from History and Theory* TB/1208

JOSE ORTEGA Y GASSET: The Modern Theme. *Introduction by Jose Ferrater Mora* TB/1038

KARL R. POPPER: The Open Society and Its Enemies
Vol. I: *The Spell of Plato* TB/1101
Vol. II: *The High Tide of Prophecy: Hegel, Marx and the Aftermath* TB/1102

KARL R. POPPER: The Poverty of Historicism [o] TB/1126

G. J. RENIER: History: Its Purpose and Method TB/1209

W. H. WALSH: Philosophy of History: *An Introduction* TB/1020

History: General

L. CARRINGTON GOODRICH: A Short History of the Chinese People. *Illus.* TB/3015

DAN N. JACOBS & HANS H. BAERWALD: Chinese Communism: *Selected Documents* TB/3031

BERNARD LEWIS: The Arabs in History TB/1029

History: Ancient

A. ANDREWES: The Greek Tyrants TB/1103

ADOLF ERMAN, Ed.: The Ancient Egyptians: *A Sourcebook of Their Writings. New material and Introduction by William Kelly Simpson* TB/1233

MICHAEL GRANT: Ancient History [o] TB/1190

SAMUEL NOAH KRAMER: Sumerian Mythology TB/1055

NAPHTALI LEWIS & MEYER REINHOLD, Eds.: Roman Civilization. *Sourcebook I: The Republic* TB/1231

NAPHTALI LEWIS & MEYER REINHOLD, Eds.: Roman Civilization. *Sourcebook II: The Empire* TB/1232

History: Medieval

P. BOISSONNADE: Life and Work in Medieval Europe: *The Evolution of the Medieval Economy, the 5th to the 15th Century.* [o] *Preface by Lynn White, Jr.* TB/1141

HELEN CAM: England before Elizabeth TB/1026

NORMAN COHN: The Pursuit of the Millennium: *Revolutionary Messianism in Medieval and Reformation Europe* TB/1037

G. G. COULTON: Medieval Village, Manor, and Monastery TB/1022

HEINRICH FICHTENAU: The Carolingian Empire: *The Age of Charlemagne* TB/1142

F. L. GANSHOF: Feudalism TB/1058

EDWARD GIBBON: The Triumph of Christendom in the Roman Empire (*Chaps. XV-XX of "Decline and Fall," J. B. Bury edition*). § *Illus.* TB/46

W. O. HASSALL, Ed.: Medieval England: *As Viewed by Contemporaries* TB/1205

DENYS HAY: The Medieval Centuries [o] TB/1192

J. M. HUSSEY: The Byzantine World TB/1057

FERDINAND LOT: The End of the Ancient World and the Beginnings of the Middle Ages. *Introduction by Glanville Downey* TB/1044

G. MOLLAT: The Popes at Avignon: 1305-1378 TB/308

CHARLES PETIT-DUTAILLIS: The Feudal Monarchy in France and England: *From the Tenth to the Thirteenth Century* [o] TB/1165

HENRI PIRENNE: Early Democracies in the Low Countries: *Urban Society and Political Conflict in the Middle Ages and the Renaissance. Introduction by John H. Mundy* TB/1110

STEVEN RUNCIMAN: A History of the Crusades.
Volume I: *The First Crusade and the Foundation of the Kingdom of Jerusalem. Illus.* TB/1143
Volume II: *The Kingdom of Jerusalem and the Frankish East, 1100-1187. Illus.* TB/1243

FERDINAND SCHEVILL: Siena: *The History of a Medieval Commune. Intro. by William M. Bowsky* TB/1164

SULPICIUS SEVERUS et al.: The Western Fathers: *Being the Lives of Martin of Tours, Ambrose, Augustine of Hippo, Honoratus of Arles and Germanus of Auxerre. Edited and translated by F. R. Hoare* TB/309

HENRY OSBORN TAYLOR: The Classical Heritage of the Middle Ages. *Foreword and Biblio. by Kenneth M. Setton* TB/1117

F. VAN DER MEER: Augustine the Bishop: *Church and Society at the Dawn of the Middle Ages* TB/304

J. M. WALLACE-HADRILL: The Barbarian West: *The Early Middle Ages, A.D. 400-1000* TB/1061

History: Modern European

L. B. NAMIER: Vanished Supremacies: *Essays on European History, 1812-1918* TB/1088

JOHN U. NEF: Western Civilization Since the Renaissance: *Peace, War, Industry, and the Arts* TB/1113

FREDERICK L. NUSSBAUM: The Triumph of Science and Reason, 1660-1685. * *Illus.* TB/3009

JOHN PLAMENATZ: German Marxism and Russian Communism. ° *New Preface by the Author* TB/1189

RAYMOND W. POSTGATE, Ed.: Revolution from 1789 to 1906: *Selected Documents* TB/1063

PENFIELD ROBERTS: The Quest for Security, 1715-1740. * *Illus.* TB/3016

PRISCILLA ROBERTSON: Revolutions of 1848: *A Social History* TB/1025

ALBERT SOREL: Europe Under the Old Regime. *Translated by Francis H. Herrick* TB/1121

N. N. SUKHANOV: The Russian Revolution, 1917: *Eyewitness Account. Edited by Joel Carmichael*
Vol. I TB/1066; Vol. II TB/1067

A. J. P. TAYLOR: The Habsburg Monarch, 1809-1918: *A History of the Austrian Empire and Austria-Hungary* ° TB/1187

JOHN B. WOLF: The Emergence of the Great Powers, 1685-1715. * *Illus.* TB/3010

JOHN B. WOLF: France: 1814-1919: *The Rise of a Liberal-Democratic Society* TB/3019

Intellectual History & History of Ideas

HERSCHEL BAKER: The Image of Man: *A Study of the Idea of Human Dignity in Classical Antiquity, the Middle Ages, and the Renaissance* TB/1047

R. R. BOLGAR: The Classical Heritage and Its Beneficiaries: *From the Carolingian Age to the End of the Renaissance* TB/1125

RANDOLPH S. BOURNE: War and the Intellectuals: *Collected Essays, 1915-1919.* ‡ *Edited by Carl Resek* TB/3043

J. BRONOWSKI & BRUCE MAZLISH: The Western Intellectual Tradition: *From Leonardo to Hegel* TB/3001

ERNST CASSIRER: The Individual and the Cosmos in Renaissance Philosophy. *Translated with an Introduction by Mario Domandi* TB/1097

NORMAN COHN: The Pursuit of the Millennium: *Revolutionary Messianism in Medieval and Reformation Europe* TB/1037

C. C. GILLISPIE: Genesis and Geology: *The Decades before Darwin* § TB/51

G. RACHEL LEVY: Religious Conceptions of the Stone Age and Their Influence upon European Thought. *Illus. Introduction by Henri Frankfort* TB/106

ARTHUR O. LOVEJOY: The Great Chain of Being: *A Study of the History of an Idea* TB/1009

FRANK E. MANUEL: The Prophets of Paris: *Turgot, Condorcet, Saint-Simon, Fourier, and Comte* TB/1218

PERRY MILLER & T. H. JOHNSON, Editors: The Puritans: *A Sourcebook of Their Writings*
Vol. I TB/1093; Vol. II TB/1094

MILTON C. NAHM: Genius and Creativity: *An Essay in the History of Ideas* TB/1196

ROBERT PAYNE: Hubris: *A Study of Pride. Foreword by Sir Herbert Read* TB/1031

RALPH BARTON PERRY: The Thought and Character of William James: *Briefer Version* TB/1156

GEORG SIMMEL et al.: Essays on Sociology, Philosophy, and Aesthetics. || *Edited by Kurt H. Wolff* TB/1234

BRUNO SNELL: The Discovery of the Mind: *The Greek Origins of European Thought* TB/1018

PAGET TOYNBEE: Dante Alighieri: *His Life and Work. Edited with Intro. by Charles S. Singleton* TB/1206

ERNEST LEE TUVESON: Millennium and Utopia: *A Study in the Background of the Idea of Progress.* || *New Preface by the Author* TB/1134

PAUL VALÉRY: The Outlook for Intelligence TB/2016

PHILIP P. WIENER: Evolution and the Founders of Pragmatism. *Foreword by John Dewey* TB/1212

Literature, Poetry, The Novel & Criticism

JAMES BAIRD: Ishmael: *The Art of Melville in the Contexts of International Primitivism* TB/1023

JACQUES BARZUN: The House of Intellect TB/1051

W. J. BATE: From Classic to Romantic: *Premises of Taste in Eighteenth Century England* TB/1036

RACHEL BESPALOFF: On the Iliad TB/2006

R. P. BLACKMUR et al.: Lectures in Criticism. *Introduction by Huntington Cairns* TB/2003

ABRAHAM CAHAN: The Rise of David Levinsky: *a documentary novel of social mobility in early twentieth century America. Intro. by John Higham* TB/1028

ERNST R. CURTIUS: European Literature and the Latin Middle Ages TB/2015

GEORGE ELIOT: Daniel Deronda: *a novel. Introduction by F. R. Leavis* TB/1039

ADOLF ERMAN, Ed.: The Ancient Egyptians: *A Sourcebook of Their Writings. New Material and Introduction by William Kelly Simpson* TB/1233

ÉTIENNE GILSON: Dante and Philosophy TB/1089

ALFRED HARBAGE: As They Liked It: *A Study of Shakespeare's Moral Artistry* TB/1035

STANLEY R. HOPPER, Ed.: Spiritual Problems in Contemporary Literature § TB/21

A. R. HUMPHREYS: The Augustan World: *Society, Thought and Letters in 18th Century England* ° TB/1105

ALDOUS HUXLEY: Antic Hay & The Giaconda Smile. ° *Introduction by Martin Green* TB/3503

ALDOUS HUXLEY: Brave New World & Brave New World Revisited. ° *Introduction by Martin Green* TB/3501

HENRY JAMES: Roderick Hudson: *a novel. Introduction by Leon Edel* TB/1016

HENRY JAMES: The Tragic Muse: *a novel. Introduction by Leon Edel* TB/1017

ARNOLD KETTLE: An Introduction to the English Novel.
Volume I: *Defoe to George Eliot* TB/1011
Volume II: *Henry James to the Present* TB/1012

ROGER SHERMAN LOOMIS: The Development of Arthurian Romance TB/1167

JOHN STUART MILL: On Bentham and Coleridge. *Introduction by F. R. Leavis* TB/1070

KENNETH B. MURDOCK: Literature and Theology in Colonial New England TB/99

SAMUEL PEPYS: The Diary of Samuel Pepys. ° *Edited by O. F. Morshead. Illus. by Ernest Shepard* TB/1007

ST.-JOHN PERSE: Seamarks TB/2002

GEORGE SANTAYANA: Interpretations of Poetry and Religion § TB/9

HEINRICH STRAUMANN: American Literature in the Twentieth Century. *Third Edition, Revised* TB/1168

PAGET TOYNBEE: Dante Alighieri: *His Life and Works. Edited with Intro. by Charles S. Singleton* TB/1206

DOROTHY VAN GHENT: The English Novel: *Form and Function* TB/1050

E. B. WHITE: One Man's Meat. *Introduction by Walter Blair* TB/3505

MORTON DAUWEN ZABEL, Editor: Literary Opinion in America Vol. I TB/3013; Vol. II TB/3014

Myth, Symbol & Folklore

JOSEPH CAMPBELL, Editor: Pagan and Christian Mysteries. *Illus.* TB/2013

MIRCEA ELIADE: Cosmos and History: *The Myth of the Eternal Return* § TB/2050

MERCEA ELIADE: Rites and Symbols of Initiation: *The Mysteries of Birth and Rebirth* § TB/1236

C. G. JUNG & C. KERÉNYI: Essays on a Science of Mythology: *The Myths of the Divine Child and the Divine Maiden* TB/2014

DORA & ERWIN PANOFSKY: Pandora's Box: *The Changing Aspects of a Mythical Symbol. Revised Edition. Illus.* TB/2021

ERWIN PANOFSKY: Studies in Iconology: *Humanistic Themes in the Art of the Renaissance. 180 illustrations* TB/1077

JEAN SEZNEC: The Survival of the Pagan Gods: *The Mythological Tradition and its Place in Renaissance Humanism and Art. 108 illustrations* TB/2004

HELLMUT WILHELM: Change: *Eight Lectures on the I Ching* TB/2019

HEINRICH ZIMMER: Myths and Symbols in Indian Art and Civilization. *70 illustrations* TB/2005

Philosophy

G. E. M. ANSCOMBE: An Introduction to Wittgenstein's Tractatus. *Second edition, Revised.* ° TB/1210

HENRI BERGSON: Time and Free Will: *An Essay on the Immediate Data of Consciousness* ° TB/1021

H. J. BLACKHAM: Six Existentialist Thinkers: *Kierkegaard, Nietzsche, Jaspers, Marcel, Heidegger, Sartre* ° TB/1002

CRANE BRINTON: Nietzsche. *New Preface, Bibliography and Epilogue by the Author* TB/1197

ERNST CASSIRER: The Individual and the Cosmos in Renaissance Philosophy. *Translated with an Introduction by Mario Domandi* TB/1097

ERNST CASSIRER: Rousseau, Kant and Goethe. *Introduction by Peter Gay* TB/1092

FREDERICK COPLESTON: Medieval Philosophy ° TB/376

F. M. CORNFORD: Principium Sapientiae: *A Study of the Origins of Greek Philosophical Thought. Edited by W. K. C. Guthrie* TB/1213

F. M. CORNFORD: From Religion to Philosophy: *A Study in the Origins of Western Speculation* § TB/20

WILFRID DESAN: The Tragic Finale: *An Essay on the Philosophy of Jean-Paul Sartre* TB/1030

A. P. D'ENTRÈVES: Natural Law: *An Historical Survey* TB/1223

HERBERT FINGARETTE: The Self in Transformation: *Psychoanalysis, Philosophy and the Life of the Spirit* ‖ TB/1177

PAUL FRIEDLÄNDER: Plato: *An Introduction* TB/2017

ÉTIENNE GILSON: Dante and Philosophy TB/1089

WILLIAM CHASE GREENE: Moira: *Fate, Good, and Evil in Greek Thought* TB/1104

W. K. C. GUTHRIE: The Greek Philosophers: *From Thales to Aristotle* ° TB/1008

F. H. HEINEMANN: Existentialism and the Modern Predicament TB/28

ISAAC HUSIK: A History of Medieval Jewish Philosophy JP/3

EDMUND HUSSERL: Phenomenology and the Crisis of Philosophy. *Translated with an Introduction by Quentin Lauer* TB/1170

IMMANUEL KANT: The Doctrine of Virtue, *being Part II of The Metaphysic of Morals. Trans. with Notes & Intro. by Mary J. Gregor. Foreword by H. J. Paton* TB/110

IMMANUEL KANT: Groundwork of the Metaphysic of Morals. *Trans. & analyzed by H. J. Paton* TB/1159

IMMANUEL KANT: Lectures on Ethics. § *Introduction by Lewis W. Beck* TB/105

IMMANUEL KANT: Religion Within the Limits of Reason Alone. § *Intro. by T. M. Greene & J. Silber* TB/67

QUENTIN LAUER: Phenomenology: *Its Genesis and Prospect* TB/1169

GABRIEL MARCEL: Being and Having: *An Existential Diary. Intro. by James Collins* TB/310

GEORGE A. MORGAN: What Nietzsche Means TB/1198

PHILO, SAADYA GAON, & JEHUDA HALEVI: Three Jewish Philosophers. *Ed. by Hans Lewy, Alexander Altmann, & Isaak Heinemann* TB/813

MICHAEL POLANYI: Personal Knowledge: *Towards a Post-Critical Philosophy* TB/1158

WILLARD VAN ORMAN QUINE: Elementary Logic: *Revised Edition* TB/577

WILLARD VAN ORMAN QUINE: From a Logical Point of View: *Logico-Philosophical Essays* TB/566

BERTRAND RUSSELL et al.: The Philosophy of Bertrand Russell. *Edited by Paul Arthur Schilpp*
Vol. I TB/1095; Vol. II TB/1096

L. S. STEBBING: A Modern Introduction to Logic TB/538

ALFRED NORTH WHITEHEAD: Process and Reality: *An Essay in Cosmology* TB/1033

PHILIP P. WIENER: Evolution and the Founders of Pragmatism. *Foreword by John Dewey* TB/1212

WILHELM WINDELBAND: A History of Philosophy
Vol. I: *Greek, Roman, Medieval* TB/38
Vol. II: *Renaissance, Enlightenment, Modern* TB/39

LUDWIG WITTGENSTEIN: The Blue and Brown Books ° TB/1211

Political Science & Government

JEREMY BENTHAM: The Handbook of Political Fallacies. *Introduction by Crane Brinton* TB/1069

KENNETH E. BOULDING: Conflict and Defense: *A General Theory* TB/3024

CRANE BRINTON: English Political Thought in the Nineteenth Century TB/1071

EDWARD S. CORWIN: American Constitutional History: *Essays edited by Alpheus T. Mason and Gerald Garvey* TB/1136

ROBERT DAHL & CHARLES E. LINDBLOM: Politics, Economics, and Welfare: *Planning and Politico-Economic Systems Resolved into Basic Social Processes* TB/3037

JOHN NEVILLE FIGGIS: The Divine Right of Kings. *Introduction by G. R. Elton* TB/1191

JOHN NEVILLE FIGGIS: Political Thought from Gerson to Grotius: 1414-1625: *Seven Studies. Introduction by Garrett Mattingly* TB/1032

F. L. GANSHOF: Feudalism TB/1058

G. P. GOOCH: English Democratic Ideas in Seventeenth Century TB/1006

J. H. HEXTER: More's Utopia: *The Biography of an Idea. New Epilogue by the Author* TB/1195

SIDNEY HOOK: Reason, Social Myths and Democracy TB/1237

ROBERT H. JACKSON: The Supreme Court in the American System of Government TB/1106

DAN N. JACOBS, Ed.: The New Communist Manifesto & *Related Documents. Third edition, Revised* TB/1078

DAN N. JACOBS & HANS BAERWALD, Eds.: Chinese Communism: *Selected Documents* TB/3031

ROBERT GREEN MCCLOSKEY: American Conservatism in the Age of Enterprise, 1865-1910 TB/1137

KINGSLEY MARTIN: French Liberal Thought in the Eighteenth Century: *Political Ideas from Bayle to Condorcet* TB/1114

ROBERTO MICHELS: First Lectures in Political Sociology. *Edited by Alfred De Grazia* ‖ ° TB/1224

JOHN STUART MILL: On Bentham and Coleridge. *Introduction by F. R. Leavis* TB/1070

BARRINGTON MOORE, JR.: Political Power and Social Theory: *Seven Studies* ‖ TB/1221

BARRINGTON MOORE, JR.: Soviet Politics—The Dilemma of Power: *The Role of Ideas in Social Change* ‖ TB/1222

JOHN B. MORRALL: Political Thought in Medieval Times TB/1076

JOHN PLAMENATZ: German Marxism and Russian Communism. ° *New Preface by the Author* TB/1189

KARL R. POPPER: The Open Society and Its Enemies
Vol. I: *The Spell of Plato* TB/1101
Vol. II: *The High Tide of Prophecy: Hegel, Marx, and the Aftermath* TB/1102

HENRI DE SAINT-SIMON: Social Organization, The Science of Man, and Other Writings. *Edited and Translated by Felix Markham* TB/1152

JOSEPH A. SCHUMPETER: Capitalism, Socialism and Democracy TB/3008

Christianity: The Roman and Eastern Traditions

Oriental Religions: Far Eastern, Near Eastern

Philosophy of Religion

Religion, Culture & Society

NATURAL SCIENCES AND MATHEMATICS

Biological Sciences